CULT FILMS

Taboo and Transgression

A Select Survey over 9 Decades

Allan Havis

University Press of America,® Inc.
Lanham · Boulder · New York · Toronto · Plymouth, UK

Copyright © 2008 by
University Press of America®, Inc.
4501 Forbes Boulevard
Suite 200
Lanham, Maryland 20706
UPA Acquisitions Department (301) 459-3366

Estover Road
Plymouth PL6 7PY
United Kingdom

Library of Congress Control Number: 2007940284
ISBN-13: 978-0-7618-3967-5 (paperback : alk. paper)
ISBN-10: 0-7618-3967-4 (paperback : alk. paper)

⊖™ The paper used in this publication meets the minimum
requirements of American National Standard for Information
Sciences—Permanence of Paper for Printed Library Materials,
ANSI Z39.48—1984

To my exceptional children,

Simone and Julian

a love of film is theirs . . .

and

a dear mentor and friend,

Robert Morris

Contents

Acknowledgements:

This book was a labor of love—without the extraordinary professional help managing a galaxy of data, text formatting, and indexing by Julie Morris—another year would have transpired without any real progress. In addition, Julie assisted the project with many rounds of smart proofreading all the while keeping a keen eye on Thurgood Marshall College Provost Office at University of California, San Diego. I would like to thank my colleague at the University of California, San Diego—Earl Warren College Provost Steven Adler—for his subtle intelligence and heartfelt generosity guiding the manuscript and giving wonderful, copious notes to the book. My thanks as well to Julia Loy, of Rowman & Littlefield Publishing Group, for essential assistance with the manuscript. Finally, I would like to praise my wife Julia for her rich patience and encouragement with this film project and for teaching cult films in my absence.

Introduction

Certainly, every cineaste has a favorite cult film that can be championed loudly late at night over bawdy laughter, hard drinks, cigarettes, and strong coffee. Was it John Waters' *Pink Flamingos* (1972)? David Lynch's *Eraserhead* (1977)? George Romero's *Night of the Living Dead* (1968)? Or loving the aging grand dames Bette Davis and Joan Crawford perversely slugging it out in *Whatever Happened to Baby Jane* (1962)? Perhaps something very recent, like the Euro-trash cabaret rock of *Hedwig and the Angry Inch* (2001) or the German made, MTV turbo-charged *Run Lola Run* (1998)? Colorful, heated arguments flow in a thousand directions. Cinematic names, song titles, and historic dates are dropped. Our memories are aroused regarding where we were physically and emotionally when we first caught Harrison Ford in *Blade Runner* (1982) or Catherine Deneuve in *Repulsion* (1965). Was it in Manhattan's dilapidated Thalia Theatre? Or Brookline's revered Plaza? Lexington's renovated 1922 "picture palace" Kentucky Theatre?[1] San Diego's indestructible Ken Cinema, burdened by the unexpected "valet parking" of border town car thieves? The self-perpetuating Yale Film Society in search of a permanent building? A nostalgia as keen and sweet as recalling our first hot teenage kiss.

What about those wild tangents and salacious gossip about the film's back story? The infamous Charles Manson attack on the family of the director of *Rosemary's Baby* (1968), the Kennedy clan suppressing the re-release of *Manchurian Candidate* (1962) until 1987, the string of supernatural accidents to the actors and crew of *The Exorcist* (1973), the accidental early deaths of grand martial artist Bruce Lee in 1973 and his son Brandon Lee during the making of *The Crow* (1993)?

No one agrees about the top selection of such benchmark films or their unnerving, mindboggling metaphors or the extremely obscure cultural allusions from the film's time period. It is a Pandora's Box blown wide open by cult enthusiasts and contrarians in fevered debate. Authoritative reference help is always desirable with regard to accurate social history, film bibliography, and the evolution of cult film aesthetics. In my many years of teaching cult films and because the divisions of cult genres was a maddening exercise in hair-splitting, a historical syllabus was born.

Concocting a vest-pocket chronology of weird cult movies made over the last nine decades should be practical, cogent, and set in a variety of interesting directions if one factors in certain aesthetic likes and necessities. Let us first rule out any archival encyclopedia for the sheer avoidance of the drudgery of cataloging. Secondly, it would be extremely helpful to differentiate two essential branches of cult films, even though both branches involve repeat film viewing. One popular branch of cult adores, worships, and scrutinizes our leading actors, performers, and celebrities such as Judy Garland, Humphrey Bogart, the Marx Brothers, Bruce Lee, The Beatles, Pee Wee Herman, Arnold Schwarzenegger, Madonna, etc. The alternate branch of cult focuses on the very nature of strange and unusual tales, fantasy films, and enormously cheap, shoddy films that would often appear in drive-in theatres across America. Many of these alternate-realm films explore knowingly or inadvertently powerful social taboos. We can define taboos in the context of social codes and anthropological phobias. Clearly, taboos of significant impact seen from two or more clashing vantage points can define a society and an era quite profoundly. Incest is prohibited throughout Western Civilization, yet European Royal families condoned it to perpetuate their bloodlines. Murder can be assumed a universal taboo, yet it is sanctioned by society in declarations of war and in the execution of a death penalty. It is this very contradiction of taboos and their transgressions that thrusts this particular and irreverent study of favorite cult films.

Lastly, this study would do well by selecting several film examples that are less famous in order to enhance this rare horizon of cinema art. This also allows us to celebrate some neglected originality found within each decade and, to a larger extent, the cascading century of cult. Therefore, the queen of all cult movies, and of costumed audience participation frenzy, of bathos, and of pansexual adulation, *The Rocky Horror Picture Show* (1975), looms too large, too famous, and unnecessarily obvious on our radar screen.

Cult films became branded in the late 1960s and flourished as a trendy, social activity for nearly twenty years. Regrettably, the genre has more application today for DVD rentals and website surfing than actual box office reality. How do we explain this odd paradoxical feeling when an excellent cult film entertains and disturbs us in the same sitting? Are we fully aware of our sacred and cherished taboos? Do we have asinine taboos? Do we assume that many cult films deliberately go slumming into bleak, unknown regions to shatter these inviolate prescriptions? Is the cult audience elite and limited in number for such seemingly rude films? Can a cult film audience be cultivated to be more naughty or less? Do an audience's age, ethnicity, and geography play a role in the process of such cultivation? Moreover, does it matter if these movies are seen in dilapidated downtown theatres (fewer and fewer each year thanks to gentrification), in hip college campus midnight showings, or in upscale, upholstered multiplexes with stadium seating and valet parking? How many people inside a room are required to create the vital sense of congregation in a proper viewing? Has the advent of premium cable, TiVo, VHS, DVD, pirate duplications, and the Internet changed forever the social consumption of cult films? And if we reflect back seventy-nine years to Luis Buñuel's radical *Un Chien Andalou* (1929), can we discern any upward evolution in style and artistry of really deranged films?

Before addressing these questions, I would like to convey a personal frisson that perhaps hits the very nerve of countless cult films. The shudder always begins with a recurring dream about boarding a flight to a foreign place; and recent fantasies have touched on this (e.g., *Fearless* [1993], *Final Destination* [2000], *Flightplan* [2005], and *Snakes on a Plane* [2006]). An unmistakable odor pervades the plane, perhaps the stench of an old movie palace's latrine? I ask the crew to let me leave in time to catch another flight. But they violently lock the door. We're now airborne. Adding to the nightmare, there is horrific turbulence, lightning, tiny liquor bottles roll down the aisles. The other passen-

gers appear remote, casual, cold. The perversely dressed, heavyset sumo wrest-
ler to my left—blocking the aisle—doesn't break the silence at my frantic questions. He takes out a long cigar and an expensive lighter. My necktie is on fire.
The jet then dives headlong into the sea. I can't hear myself scream. Rock music
with a heavy bass blasts from someone's discarded headphones. Am I inside a
cult movie? Is the movie inside me? This sensation is a short, seductive step into
the artistic conceit behind the Pirandellian cult film *Being John Malkovich*
(1999). According to theorist and novelist Umberto Eco, many cult films and the
archetypes found within provoke in the viewer "a sort of intense emotion accompanied by the vague feeling of a *déjà vu* that everybody yearns to see
again."[2]

The cult viewer slips beyond the usual ways of seeing, sensing, and empa-
thizing with the visual story and the film's characters. The cult viewer maneuv-
ers between a comfortable distance from the film and full submersion down an
aesthetic rabbit hole. Indeed, one face that could serve as a poster-child for the
cult filmgoer is Lewis Carroll's *Alice*. One detects a modest sign of disdain and
disquietude in her otherwise placid countenance. It is both the uncertainty of
Alice's existence and of her remote sexual awareness. This concept was explored in the bacchanal of the 1960s and 1970s, when film viewing and the
rampant use of recreational drugs comingled indelibly. Further, personal protest
mixed naturally with political street protest in the wave of a sexual and racial
activism. Anecdotally, virginity was lost irrevocably in smoky theatre balconies.
Regardless of the period, however, the cult filmgoer tacitly elects to leave familiar territories of culture, home, friends, safety, and good taste. The viewer also
knows and hopes that by the end of the offbeat film he is free to return to the
reassuring reality he temporarily abandoned. Another way to express this guilt-
less "escape and return" is to allow the film participant an alter ego, an unre-
pressed secret identity, an amoral *doppelgänger*. The cult filmgoer half suspects
this truth and may even whisper it aloud, but dare he call it his true "Other"?

In a casual, cursory portrait of the "other," let us tap at the door of decadence apropos these subversive films. Culturally, decadence reflects the concept
that there are epochs in art when, after magnificent achievements and innovations, a fashionable degeneration begins among artists, exposing a putrid, final
stage of living for a leading nation. The telling, exhibitionist lives and deaths of
iconoclastic de Sade and John Waters' transvestite diva Divine embody the
metaphor of debauchery through such unpleasant illness and death. In 1770,
Voltaire wrote to a friend with the admonition: "Don't hope to regain good taste;
we are in a time of the most horrible decadence."[3] Decadence has always served
as incontestable evidence of society's desertion from morality irrespective of the
motives for desertion (e.g., indulgence, repudiation, weakness, nausea, self-
hatred, loss of faith). Another perspective on cult films' impeccable embrace of
decadence may be found in the oft-quoted maxim by Picasso that "art is the lie
which leads to truth."[4] Naturally, some would argue that truth is fashion while
others would contest that fashion is truth. Yet such is the perverse nature of art
and the delectable tyranny of fashion once the standards of a community are
offended. Hence, in the bizarre films of Tod Browning, Russ Meyer, Alejandro

Jodorowsky, John Waters, and David Lynch, is decadence a theatrical pose or a core element of human existence? Some critics would argue that for these directors, among countless others in the world of cult, it is a little of both, and the question is really of degree, of politics, of exploitation, and—of considerable importance—casting.

There is risk to the aesthetic investigation of cult films' familiar rowdy and unsavory reputation. When does the identity of the decadent become interchangeable with things relentlessly perverted and morbid to the extreme? Is it safer that our search become an inquiry into the relative banality and lineage of reprehensible Homo sapiens behavior, or is it far better to assume a neutral stance toward revolting spectacles on a large silver screen? The idea, essentially, is not one of feigning a chic indifference or an elite absence of judgment, but accepting as film viewers that our involuntary defenses frequently injure our paths toward revelation and self-discovery.

In conclusion, when one delves into the stratified essence of cult films in all their paradoxical glory, the heart of it is in the hyperbolic hue of distinguished central portraits and their destinies. The films' heroes, villains, and anti-heroes are anything but normal; plots more obscure or absurd or kinky, very often more chaotic than comfortable; social and sexually shocking themes upend tired genres, clichés, and formulas.

Sitting high up in the balcony inside this seedy cinema theatre? Hold on to your seats. It is going to be a very strange, exotic ride.

Notes

1.   Gregory A. Waller, *The Cult Film Experience*, ed. J. P. Telotte (Austin: University of Texas Press, 1991), 168-169.

2.   Umberto Eco, *Travels in Hypereality* (San Diego, New York, London: Harcourt Brace Jovanovich, 1986), 200.

3.   Richard Gilman, *Decadence: The Strange Life of an Epithet* (New York: Farrar, Straus and Giroux), 75.

4.   Gilman, *Decadence: The Strange Life of an Epithet*, 161.

Chapter One
Films from the 1920s

It would be inviting and dexterous to classify the 1920s as reactionary to preceding decades and Victorian ideals, but the fascinating trends and behavior of the period pushed American life boldly toward the bright, unruly Age of Jazz, uninhibited dancing flappers, the great Harlem Renaissance, the inadvertent glamorization of organized crime and speakeasy society under the cloud of Prohibition, and the powerful growing presence of commercial radio and film. Aptly named "The Roaring Twenties," this epoch also featured the seminal influence of the dramatic Scopes trial in Tennessee and the dominant new role of Darwin in our schools and scientific literature.

The decade began with the vital passage of the 19th Amendment granting women the right to vote; the suffrage movement reached a pinnacle of triumph. World War I had defined much of the previous decade, but the 1920s bore the difficult adjustments of a newly configured world and an unfolding revolution in Russia. Republican Calvin Coolidge won the White House in 1924, maintained a strong pro-business profile, and continued the upper class policies of his predecessor, Warren Harding. Although Prohibition stopped the legal sale and tapered the consumption of alcohol publicly, the 1920s flourished with a spontaneous flouting of the laws by private clubs and "backwater stills" in homes and farms in every state of the nation. Perhaps Prohibition provided the metaphor for the decade's major human contradiction: a public showing of temperance masking a wild appetite for heightened pleasures and the forbidden.

The 1920s celebrated wildly individualistic heroes such as magician Harry Houdini, baseball slugger Babe Ruth, and aviator Charles Lindbergh crossing the Atlantic in a small, unsafe aircraft. Lindbergh, victimized by a kidnapping, will return under a horrid lens to the public eye again in the next decade.

The literature of the period was represented by artists such as John Dos Passos, Henry Miller, William Faulkner, F. Scott Fitzgerald, Edna St. Vincent Millay, W.E.B. Du Bois, T.S. Eliot, Eugene O'Neill, Dorothy Parker, and George S. Kaufman.

In 1927, Warner Brothers produced the first film acknowledged to feature some synchronized dialogue—Alan Crosland's *The Jazz Singer*, starring Al Jolson. This achievement opened the gate to a new dimension of cinematic art. By the end of the decade, many "talkies" surfaced causing the luminous silent era films stars deep anxiety about their continued popularity and their respective ability to cross over into spoken cinematic artistry. The act of hearing a performer's speech on screen took on a realm of penetrating intimacy. Without a doubt, each film star maintained an enigmatic profile as long as the public was kept from hearing the actor's true voice. Be it Rudolf Valentino or Lilian Gish, the language in sound and gesture was once considered the personal providence of the stage artist—and only the stage artist. Before 1927, "dialogue boxes" and "captions" provided the only verbal nexus to our film stars. Decisively, Charlie Chaplin—that consummate mime and director—had been hard pressed by this conundrum of vocal expression. He took an extremely long time to adapt to the changing times, leading to his awkward paean to the silent artist, featuring himself and Buster Keaton in *Limelight* (1951).

So many stellar films were part of the 1920s that it is tempting to embrace a good number of these titles under a "cult film" banner because of their lasting importance in cinematic history and their idiosyncratic greatness: Chaplin's *The Gold Rush* (1925), Keaton's *The General* (1927), D.W. Griffith's *Birth of a Nation* (1915), Douglas Fairbanks' *The Thief of Bagdad* (1924), G. W. Pabst's *Pandora's Box* (1929), F.W. Murnau's *Sunrise* (1927), Erich von Stroheim's *Greed* (1924), Abel Gance's *Napoleon* (1927), Carl Theodor Dreyer's *La Passion de Jeanne d'Arc* (1928), Sergei Eisenstein's *Battleship Potemkin* (1925), René Clair's *The Italian Straw Hat* (1927), and Alfred Hitchcock's *The Lodger* (1927). Further, many of these films contain elements of transgression and offbeat sensationalism that would push the argument for inclusion if this were an encyclopedic book.

Phantom of the Opera (1925)

The immediate association one would make today when hearing the title—*The Phantom of the Opera*—is the Andrew Lloyd Webber smash musical, which seems unfortunate to the considerable pedigree behind the silent cinema man who wears the sinister mask. In the course of eighty years, *The Phantom of the Opera* has been realized for film an astounding six times (seven if one counts Brian De Palma's 1974 freestyle rock adaptation—*Phantom of the Paradise*), but critics universally declare the Rupert Julian's 1925 silent version as the definitive one and undoubtedly the most legendary. No secret prevails as to the reason why. Lon Chaney—the man of a thousand faces—personifies the opera monster as though Heaven itself had mandated the preternatural casting.

The role of a disfigured artist certainly was tailored for Chaney and his superlative ability, no matter the pain or the cost, to transform physically. Despite all the melodramatic trappings of the script, the dialogue cards, the lumbering film pace, and the Phantom's late entrance a third of the way into the story, Chaney infuses every moment of screen time with equal dollops of particularization, pathos, and panache. Chaney's classic performance and the magnitude of this big budget Universal Studios production created history's first great feature length horror film.

The original novel (1911) by Gaston Leroux suggests that this vengeful, mad composer actually lived beneath the Paris Opera house.[1] Taking Leroux at his word, the Phantom's desolation was grounded in reality thirty years prior to the novel and his Opera House mischief brought hell to others. The Phantom's biographical fact alone is quite tantalizing for any historic cult film.

Lon Chaney was widely known to endure limitless suffering in his many amazing impersonations. This occasion had role and actor merging perfectly. With *Phantom*, Chaney forced fishhooks and putty into his cheeks, squeezed disks up his nose, applied non-optical chemicals to shrink his pupils—anything to deliver skeletal dimension to this forbidden face.[2] Like a magician, Chaney never revealed his phenomenal make-up tricks to the public. The star, a child of deaf parents, had imbued his character with such expressive mystique and dire restlessness that audiences everywhere recoiled. Chaney's artistry in this film can be described twofold. Limited by a mask for almost half his appearance, the silent actor projected much of his emotional vitality through understated gesture and sustained eye contact. Secondly, his conviction scene for scene, from first entrance to his death, proved terribly authentic while resisting loud traces of sentimentality and self-dramatization.

Chaney, freshly riding the success of Universal's *The Hunchback of Notre Dame*, was careful to pick the next Hollywood vehicle to ratchet his career even higher. Director Rupert Julian (who also acted) demanded that Universal hire Chaney again in spite of any competitive studio interference. As an actor Julian had worked with Chaney in previous films, which granted Julian no real advantage with Chaney. Undocumented reports about the turbulent production and the imperial manner of Julian's stewardship hint that Chaney filled in for Julian with some scene direction. Worse still, actor and director fought constantly in light of Chaney's overwhelming identification with the demonic role of Erik the Phantom.[3]

To his credit, Julian went ahead to recreate the opulent, wonderful interiors of Paris Opera along with the endless catacombs of breathtaking scale. It is interesting to note that many sections of the black and white movie were filmed using the rudimentary two-color Technicolor process. However, such tinted footage no longer has survived except for the well regarded Bal Masqué scenes. There were vast amounts of script revisions and costly, obligatory post-production footage. Various endings were tacked on along the way at the bequest of producer Carl Laemmle, which brought in comedy director Edward Sedgwick like a relief pitcher and other late entry artistic participants.[4]

Director Julian was unhampered at the onset by studio financial restraints and schedules, but circumstances changed to everyone's chagrin. Clearly, the long, positive affiliation that Julian had with Universal was strained at the conclusion of filming. Production costs surpassed $600,000 (quite high for a silent feature) which included roughly $50,000 in retakes. Further, according to some heartfelt industry conjecture, the film's greatest hardship could be traced to the "jinx" generated by the story's real life Phantom. Hollywood "curses" have plagued many renowned productions; a half century after *Phantom*, *Rosemary's Baby* (1968), and *The Exorcist* (1973) have endured such "curses" with personal calamities and death to cast, crew, and their families. Nonetheless, Julian's fabulous *Phantom* brought the studio a tidy profit over half a million dollars and the prestige of well reviewed book-to-film debut.

The drama of *Phantom* entails the mysterious soul who haunts France's most esteemed performing arts house from up high Box 5. He taunts the Paris

Opera officials to promote understudy Christine over the reigning diva Carlotta. Is the Phantom evil, insane, or simply driven by human obsession? Carlotta is stricken by a sudden illness allowing Christine to go on in triumph. More warnings occur, unheeded. Carlotta returns in *Faust*. Lights flicker. A magnificent chandelier falls over the audience. Christine is abducted by the Phantom and forced to accompany him to his underground lair. While he is distracted at the organ—her hands to his face—she unveils him. Along with Christine, we are stunned beyond measure by the bone nakedness of the Phantom's deformity. His hideousness surpasses our expectations. Still, he offers his love to her. Overcoming the various diabolic traps in the Phantom's underworld, the authorities and Christine's fiancé free her.

The richness of the film's horror blending with an engaging gothic romance makes *Phantom* fully delectable for cult viewers and horror fans. The unfailing recipe of sex and death, secrecy and spectacle, genius and insanity proved to be irresistible to generations of audiences. Yet despite larger budgets and advances in movie technology, none of the subsequent *Phantom* films can rival Chaney's elemental truth and stature behind the Phantom's disguise. No remake convincingly expressed the rarefied need for this "public" character to hide from sincere recognition. The contradiction becomes unbearable to the Phantom's captive. Then again, the taboo of removing someone's psychic mask, implicit throughout the narrative, could not be any plainer to Christine. She approaches the dare gingerly but inevitably just as if she were Eve picking the forbidden apple. The action, both lyrical and clichéd, approximates sexual union or a shared collective death wish with poor Phantom Erik. Once captive of the Phantom, the young woman singer cannot resist temptation.

Film histories have cited innumerable times the consummate scene in which Christine exposes the Phantom as the most frightening screen event of its time. Hundreds upon hundreds of people had fainted in theatres. Yet, the Phantom was not supernatural like Dracula, Frankenstein's monster, or the Wolf Man. He was intensely mortal, riddled by rage, and morally twisted. So misunderstood and despised by Paris and the cognoscenti, Erik proved to be a world class hermit. Worse still for us, under his mask was nothing less than the fear of discerning his acid visage lurking atop our own in one's private mirror.

Metropolis (1926)

A towering film achievement in visual design, utter dark fantasy, and poetic futurism, Fritz Lang's *Metropolis* (1926) stands unchallenged as the first outstanding film of science fiction. Based on the novel by Thea von Harbou and produced lavishly in Germany utilizing approximately 25,000 extras on gargantuan stage sets, *Metropolis* demonstrates both the seductiveness and perils of German Expressionism. Lang's ease with stark camera angles, striking shadows, gloriously far-reaching facades, and a thrilling realization of a world fully mechanized enables the film to overcome what many critics have called a weak, implausible plot wedded to a monotonously bleak theme.

As Lang completed his first journey to America aboard an ocean liner cruise in 1924, he found himself alone on the deck taking in the glorious New York waterfront, except for another passenger—film producer Erich Pommer. Neither Pommer nor Lang was allowed to disembark due to nonresident status— a coincidence and a disappointment at first. But looking at the looming towers lit by the city's great pride, Lang imagined with perfect clarity the sculptural world of *Metropolis*. Although Lang came to repudiate the story content of the film, he remained attached to the overall design and visual artistry of the project.[5]

Lang's vision projected ahead three generations to the distant year 2000 where the affluent dominate high above in opulent, vertiginous skyscrapers. The story's essential conflict arises from the earthbound worker-slaves, thoroughly demoralized by their meaningless chores. To savvy political eyes, the illustration is a glaringly transparent Marxist trope. To Lang, years later, the symbolism was too strong.[6]

Metropolis has a hero: Freder, the spoiled son of Fredersen who rules among the elite. Lovely Maria from the subterranean world unsettles Freder at their first encounter. Poetically and literally, a romantic chord can be heard. Soon Freder, in disguise, finds himself stunned by the workers' atrocious conditions. The film revolves on this point. Freder becomes politicized at the expense of provoking Rottwang—the capitalist monster and the film's requisite villain. In retaliation, Rottwang's scheme plays out effortlessly, and he provided future science fiction films a foolproof gambit: to devise a facsimile of one's enemy (using sorcery or a neon laboratory) to deceive everyone and conquer from within. So we now have two Marias rendered masterfully by actress Brigitte Helm. While the genuine Maria is held hostage, the artificial Maria will serve as an evil "St. Joan" who discovers the hypnotic power to rouse the masses. Great pandemonium ensues. The world tumbles into total chaos. The ruling Frederson manages to rethink his political views: "perhaps it would be better to enhance the lives of the downtrodden."

The very notion of a human duplicate in *Metropolis* typifies cult film's unapologetic affection for *doppelgängers* and the inherent philosophical ramifications of a mirrored identity. There are myriad complications that bind the double and its real life analogue, or that bind biological twins for that matter. Indeed, the very idea fuels the psychological films of Bergman's *Persona* (1966), Kieslowski's *The Double Life of Véronique* (1991), and Cronenberg's *Dead Ringers* (1994). As for Maria and her wicked double, *Metropolis* makes far too much of one individual's role in igniting a revolution. Perhaps Lang was enamored of a famous Hegelian belief that one exceptional individual in every century can turn the pages of history forward. Because of Maria's utter commonness and her spectacular transformation, Fritz Lang's narrative conceit assumes a comic book touch. Theatrically, Maria's face is lifted to dress an automaton. The taboo of identity theft falls short of the crime of murder yet the damage of such theft can be catastrophic. Certainly that is the instance within *Metropolis*. One of Lang's leading cinematic themes concerns what occurs when the social machine explodes after an initial incident of violence. He pursued this theme again to great effect in a disquieting cult film about a hunted child molester (the haunted Peter Lorrie) titled by the single letter *M* (1931). The excitement behind Lang's sensibility informs so many subsequent and contemporary cult classics.

If *Metropolis* can be faulted for sacrificing character depth to benefit spectacle and for its lumbering action sequences, perhaps we are missing the perspective of the film's profundity. *Metropolis* brings into thematic play aspects of hieroglyphics interconnected with the tower of Babel formalities.[7] The film unlocks a frightful, dream world which stretches and contorts empirical reality. Lang's aggressive cameras escort us inside the power plant; we witness the workers maneuvering the hands of a gigantic clock. But within this nightmare life, machinery will fail and humanity will be tortured.

The stirring special effects and optical treats were the work of visual artist Eugene Schuefftan and cinematographer Karl Freund. Schuefttan's amazing miniature models would soon influence enormously the filmmakers in America. If we judge this film on its own terms and in its own time, how can we not be moved by Lang's achievement? Yes, the images are extremely grotesque and exaggerated; the mechanization of our future world often appears unrealistic. The vast array of technical and architectural talents who built *Metropolis* discovered a uniform look and feel consistent with the accelerated age of science in the 1920s. Considered by many as the most pungent visual images in Lang's world is Freder's stark perception of the god of human sacrifice, Moloch, in the machine room after one of the instruments explodes.[8] Politics inhabit the inside of the film along with the distinct ideological life of it in Germany. Adolf Hitler was one of *Metropolis*'s early admirers and tried to enlist Lang to join his propaganda wing. Lang was so disturbed by Hitler's attempt to co-opt his talents that he abruptly left for Los Angeles to make a handful of Hollywood films including *The Big Heat* (1953) and *Rancho Notorious* (1952).

Colossal *Metropolis* suffered from sizable edits from philistine censors and distributors over the long years. A newly edited version compiled by Giorgio Moroder that added "lost" footage from Germany and Austria was shown in 1984. The Moroder copy also colorized the film stock with the public explanation that Lang had wanted color all along. The controversial artistic sabotage of colorizing classic black and white films has had a full media debate, triggered in the early 1980s by Ted Turner's cable networks and licensing. Of course, TV ratings had determined that colorizing classic films raked in a larger audience.

Not enough can be said on the prescient nature of *Metropolis*'s vision of a contorted utopia. Still photos from the film burn into our subconscious. A fine array of postmodern architects was aroused, perplexed, and intoxicated by the film's style. Dozens of cult films owe a tremendous deal to Lang's dreamscape: George Miller's *Road Warrior* (1981), Ridley Scott's *Blade Runner* (1982), Godard's *Alphaville* (1965), and John Carpenter's *Escape from New York* (1981). Even in this new millennium, *Metropolis* offers us a disturbing parallel universe that pits tomorrow's unknown reality against machines and artificial intelligence.

Un Chien Andalou (1929)

Invariably, the cinematic annals of the avant-garde lead back to a little surreal project of Luis Buñuel and Salvador Dalí in 1929 that has tweaked the sophisticated world with lasting effect. *Un Chien Andalou (*The Andalusian Dog*)* was chiefly funded by Buñuel's affluent mother, but that did not stop countries from banning her son's film. Due to an unhappy distribution problem that arose from its nauseating, illogical content, *Un Chien Andalou*, a sly, shocking seventeen-minute film, was viewed only at private clubs or in the studios of friends and surrealists. For a silent film of this brevity to have such powerful influence worldwide was quite astounding. When mentioning the film even today, the scene most cited is the notorious slitting of a woman's eye with a shaving razor. No computer simulation there; a dead donkey's organ was employed for the breathless, special effect. The Parisian filmgoer in 1929 had no idea that this enacted violence would come so randomly, so suddenly, in the film, and so absent of moral judgment.

Buñuel went on to make feature films of great importance and controversy, such as *Le Charme Discret de la Bourgeoisie* (The Discreet Charm of the Bourgeoisie) (1972) and *Belle de Jour* (1967). Buñuel, a Spaniard by birth, found his artistic home in Paris for much of his life, although after the Spanish Civil war, he found refuge in Mexico from 1946 -1961. Throughout his life, Buñuel had a phenomenal affinity toward the morbid and the surreal. Perhaps perversity was the only path of personal truth and wit for this nuanced filmmaker. One could explain Salvador Dalí's decadent sensibility in similar fashion. Adding to the developing tensions between Buñuel and Dalí was Dalí's wife Gala Dalí. She and Buñuel antagonized each other so much that in 1929, at a country picnic, Buñuel found himself on the ground with his hands around her throat. Fifty years later, Buñuel dreamed that Gala sat in a theatre and kissed him lovingly on the lips.[9] More seriously, two decades after *L'Âge d'Or* (1930) when Dalí curiously worked his way back to the Catholic Church and to the regime of Spain's Franco, the painter broke from Buñuel and Buñuel's surrealist manifesto.

The feature films of Buñuel demonstrated sufficient obligation to tell a concrete story and to adhere to some degree of human logic and longing. However, *Un Chien Andalou* unfolds like a silent, persistent dream built upon disconcerting images (and in some versions, accompanied by incongruous music from a Wagner opera and the popular tango). After the slitting of a human eye, we see the graceful movement of horizontal clouds gliding across a full moon. A woman witnesses a man, wearing a Dutch maid's hat, riding a bicycle. Suddenly he dies. A crowd forms. A severed hand is placed inside a wood box. Later, the dead man visits her apartment in hopes of having sex with the woman. Inexplicably, the man kills what appears to be his "double." The startled woman flees, and we see her on a deserted beach where she, to her satisfaction, finds another man. Another jump: the woman and man are buried to their midsections like hapless characters from a 1960s Beckett play. Clearly, the sequence of events invites artistic speculation and macabre laughter, and for those not "in on the joke," the film generates a good dose of disturbance and discomfort.

The ensuing scandal in Paris that was *Un Chien Andalou* was quite real. At the film's Studio des Ursulines premiere with Picasso, Le Corbusier, Cocteau and other notable artists and surrealists in attendance, Buñuel alleged in his autobiography to have hidden himself with stones in his pockets ready to toss at the protesting audience.[10] That evening, he was a nervous wreck, saddled by musical obligations all the while; behind the screen Buñuel was operating the record player, alternating Argentinean tangos with Wagner's *Tristan und Isolde*.

Influential to Buñuel during this period were the following films that he went on to present at a lecture in Madrid: René Clair's *Entr'acte* (1924), Jean Renoir's *La Fille de L'eau* (1925), and Cavalcanti's *Rien ou les Heures* (1926). Buñuel was dismayed by the aristocratic audience in Spain and felt compelled to suggest to the lecture society administrator that there be a menstruation contest with awarded prizes after the finale (so much for Buñuel's delicate sensibility to his native land).

During an overnight visit to Dalí's home in Figueras, Spain, Buñuel talked about a dream featuring a long, tapered cloud that sliced the moon like a razor through an eye. Dalí replied that he had recently dreamed of a hand crawling with ants. This was the genesis of their composition. Buñuel and Dalí finished writing *Un Chien Andalou* in less than a week. Their only creative rule was that no idea or image susceptible to reasoning would be allowed. As Buñuel attests in his writings, no argument had passed between Dalí and Buñuel during the birthing of the script. Half the money Buñuel's mother provided for the film was blown on Buñuel's dalliances at nightclubs. Remarkably, the film took two weeks to shoot, using just a handful of people. It was a chance occasion with photographer Man Ray that prompted Buñuel to debut the secret film. Had Ray not been persuaded by Buñuel's gentle salesmanship of *Un Chien Andalou*, one wonders if the film would have gone public at all. The film convinced Buñuel that there was no way he would ever make a commercial entertainment.[11]

If today's audiences are less offended by *Un Chien Andalou* we should not be terribly surprised. Thousands of subsequent films around the globe have pushed shock and violence to levels exceeding Buñuel's visions. Perhaps Buñuel and Dalí have succeeded in their young men's quest to goad the dull bourgeois mind. This uncanny silent film was nurtured from the dark well of Buñuel and Dalí's unconscious. It was their mad, collective intimacy that would inspire them to make another short dream-film, *L'Âge d'Or*, the following year, financed by high society leader Le Vicomte. *L'Âge d'Or* was condemned by the Catholic Church for unchecked sacrilege and sparked extreme right-wingers to tear the seats apart in the cinema. Like *Un Chien Andalou*, *L'Âge d'Or* was banned in many neighboring countries. Today, these two titles are often shown together as a full evening's fare—without riots.

Dalí returned to painting, but participated again in film with an assignment for Alfred Hitchcock's production of *Spellbound*—the abstract dream sequence that earned an Oscar in 1945. Buñuel proceeded to execute uninspired chores for MGM, overseeing Spanish versions of Hollywood releases, before his Mexican detour making curious B films. He enjoyed an international success in 1961 with *Viridiana*, about the life of a nun who loses her innocence. In 1983, he published a devious autobiography, *My Last Sigh*, which pleased book critics universally. Luis Buñuel's peculiar creativity and commercial luck improved greatly in the two decades that followed with these masterworks of *Viridiana*, *The Exterminating Angel* (El Ángel Exterminador) (1962), *Diary of a Chambermaid* (Le Journal d'une Femme de Chambre) (1964), and *Tristana* (1970).

Notes:

1.   Jerrold E Hogle, *The Undergrounds of the Phantom of the Opera* (New York and Hampshire, England: Palgrave, 2002), 3.

2.   Hogle, *The Undergrounds of the Phantom of the Opera*, 138.

3.   Hogle, *The Undergrounds of the Phantom of the Opera*, 138.

4.   Philip J. Riley, *Phantom of the Opera (Hollywood Archives Series)* (Absecon, New Jersey: MagicImage Filmbooks, 1999), 208.

5.   Fritz Lang and Barry Keith Grant, *Fritz Lang: Interviews (Conversations with Filmmakers)* (Oxford, Mississippi: University Press of Mississippi, 2003), 12.

6.   Lang and Grant, *Fritz Lang: Interviews (Conversations with Filmmakers)*, 3.

7.   Tom Gunning, *The Films of Fritz Lang* (London: British Film Institute, 2000), 56.

8.   Gunning, *The Films of Fritz Lang*, 8.

9.   Luis Buñuel, *My Last Sigh: The Autobiography of Luis Buñuel* (New York: Vintage Books, 1984), 95-97.

10.   Buñuel, *My Last Sigh: The Autobiography of Luis Buñuel*, 106.

11.   Buñuel, *My Last Sigh: The Autobiography of Luis Buñuel*, 114.

Chapter Two
Films from the 1930s

American culture in the 1930s was inescapably linked to the Great Depression, a time of incomparable social and economic trauma. That period's hardship began with the spectacular stock market crash in 1929, and the ruinous spillage cascaded in the following years. The hopelessness of our nation in the early 1930s permanently scarred millions of people. What was once the dream of prosperity became the nightmare of hunger and destitution. Dust bowl farmers gambled their lives on a final push westward to California. The average annual salary at that time was $1,368 and milk cost 14 cents a quart. Shanty towns named Hoovervilles sprung up in every corner of the 48 states; President Hoover believed financial aid had to come from the private sector. Still, young people danced to fabulous big bands and Hoover's compassionate, elegant successor, Franklin Roosevelt, calmed Americans with his famous Fireside Chats. The workers' union movement became more visible and widespread well into the decade. Still, the nation was uncertain about both the decisions ahead and the basic health and survival of the family. Europe fared no better as several democracies degenerated into tyrannies. Movies, radio, pulp mystery books, baseball, and board games held the country's attention.

The era featured Father Charles E. Coughlin, a cultish radio personality who, at the height of his popularity, boasted he had 30 million impassioned listeners. Coughlin, a Catholic priest at war with the progressive views of "international banking," questioned changing moral codes of the day, and associated a broad range of Jews with the Communist Party. Radio entertainment, thoroughly universal and ubiquitous, ran the gamut from Jack Benny to Amos 'n Andy. Serial radio hooked both the young and the old with the comic book heroics of the Green Hornet and the Lone Ranger. Perhaps the quintessential radio broadcast came on October 20, 1938, when Orson Welles aired H.G. Wells' science fiction classic *The War of the Worlds*. Over a million listeners assumed that the radio drama was an actual news alert, and the broadcast created enormous pandemonium. Thousands of listeners were prepared to die at the hands of an alien invasion from Mars.

Many of the country's commanding skyscrapers, such as the Empire State Building (*King Kong* in 1933) and the Chrysler Building, were inaugurated in the early 1930s. The classic reading primer, *Dick and Jane*, was first published in 1931—around the same time as Gertrude Stein's lean, absurd poetry. "Look. See Dick. See Dick run." Distinguished literary artists such as F. Scott Fitzgerald, Ernest Hemingway, Richard Wright, John Steinbeck, Zora Neale Hurston, Thornton Wilder, Carl Sandburg, Wallace Stevens, and John Dos Passos lent the decade a forceful profile. The middle of the decade presented the groundbreaking American folk opera *Porgy and Bess* by George Gershwin. Duke Ellington, Johnny Mercer, Irving Berlin, Benny Goodman, and Richard Rodgers added to the grand music of the time.

The explosion of fine American films from this Depression era, considered by many in the industry as Hollywood's "Golden Age," created the impression that Hollywood was immune to the economic downtown. Gangster films were much in vogue and James Cagney had no qualms about smashing a ripe grapefruit into actress Mae Clarke's face in *Public Enemy* (1931). Glamour, diffidence, and sex appeal were refined in this new chapter of talking films with the likes of Clark Gable and Greta Garbo. The Marx Brothers, powered by George Kaufman and other literate screenwriters, brought a new level of intellectual vaudeville and political zaniness to the screen. The beloved cynicism of W.C. Fields and the libidinous innuendo of Mae West shoved comedy to more outrageous boundaries. Dance and musical movies were always in demand; Busby Berkeley's imprimatur topped all film choreographers of the period. America had fallen head over heels for dimpled child star Shirley Temple as she sang and danced "The Good Ship Lollipop." In 1937 Walt Disney created his first feature animation, the technically advanced, fanciful, and spellbinding *Snow White and the Seven Dwarfs*.

As the decade concluded, grave concern was directed toward the growing crisis in Germany and her surrounding nations. Jewish genocide had entered some sphere of the public's knowledge. The Third Reich's design on Europe became paramount and irreversible. Hitler's nation had undertaken a radical transformation leading to cataclysmic actions on both sides of the Atlantic Ocean. In Asia, Japan appeared as militaristic as Germany, and Stalin's sluggish Russia was braced for the unthinkable. Mussolini's Italy joined the axis with Hitler. World War II was only moments away from erupting.

Freaks (1932)

Without question, the most telling scene found in the pioneer landmark film on human grotesqueness and outcast misfortune, Tod Browning's *Freaks*, must be the bizarre wedding banquet where all the assembled circus freaks begin chanting to the villainous blonde, Cleopatra, that she is now one of them. The garbled chant, "gobble, gobble, we accept you!" is both hypnotic to its arrogant victim and humiliating. In her anger and hysteria, Cleopatra hurls stinging insults back at the knowing, sideshow wedding guests. To all eyes and ears, she is revealed to be horribly vain and evil. Of course, she is marrying little Hans for his inheritance and his social blindness. The curious threshold between normality and abnormality, beauty and distortion, decency and indecency become discernible and irreversible in this harrowing carnival film. Moreover, of the many taboos explored within the story, none is sharper or more indelicate than the symbolic miscegenation between an attractive, full-size woman and a dwarf. Far from being an ignoble, contemporary variation of the fabled *Beauty and the Beast*

(1946), this fraudulent union upsets all fragments of society within the film and also Browning's Depression-era audience—seven years before the fabled Munchkins from Oz appeared on screen.

There are fascinating parallels to be found four decades later in macabre films that showcase without special effects malformed and monstrous anatomies: Werner Herzog's *Even Dwarfs Started Small* (1970), Federico Fellini's *Satyricon* (1970), and Alejandro Jodorowsky's *El Topo* (1971). What is evident among the aforementioned titles is the uncanny visual pathos found within and throughout each cinematic narrative—an explicit debt to Browning's cinema. Rather than allow an audience the safe shelter of a very costumed and tame fairy tale, these subsequent international directors embraced the disturbance of deformity, giving their audience wild transport to a dimension first chartered by Browning. The freaks' taunting choral chant at the wedding banquet chills as a contemporary reference nearly independent from the film—"We accept you, one of us, one of us!"[1]

When he was a child, Tod Browning had followed one of the most perfect boyhood fantasies—to quit school and join the circus.[2] He had a powerful affinity and sympathy for the peripheral carnival attractions. Previous to *Freaks*, Browning had directed the revered and renowned *Dracula* (1931), which featured Bela Lugosi. Unlike F.W. Murnau's *Nosferatu* (1922)—the classic forerunner of all vampire films—Browning's version generated countless melodramatic knockoffs of the suave Transylvanian count in swirling cape. Crediting Lugosi's grand interpration of the role and the unmistakable lyricism of the vampire legend, the Browning film chilled and thrilled millions of viewers. Still, there was something artificial and self-conscious at the heart of *Dracula* that set it apart from the mysterious and naked morbidity seen in nearly every frame of *Freaks*. For all of *Dracula*'s dramatic power, the story unfolds like a well behaved fairy tale ensconced inside a diorama.

The story of *Freaks* is relatively uncomplicated. Browning's film commences with a circus barker presenting the Feathered Hen and her sorrowful story. She was once a lovely trapeze star in Madame Tetralini's show. Her stage name was Cleopatra—"the peacock of the air"—and she tempted a German midget named Hans who was coming into a family fortune. Hans' dwarf fiancée, Frieda, suffers quietly and warns him to no avail.

Hardly a secret to the circus troupe, Hercules—the strongman—and Cleopatra are having an affair while mocking Hans' infatuation with Cleopatra. She concocts a scheme to marry Hans and steal his money. Soon the nuptial banquet is upon them. It is the overture of Cleopatra's humiliation. After getting Han's inheritance, Cleopatra introduces a diet of poison to heal an ailing bridegroom. Hans is tipped off about the plot and confronts Cleopatra. At the same time, Hercules forces himself on a former carnival girlfriend Venus. Following a fight that causes Venus' wagon to flip over, Hercules is thrown to the ground and is pursued by a posse of freaks. Other freaks surround Cleopatra. They know she was trying to kill Hans and they plan to exact revenge. Her mutilation, so hideous and permanent, is beyond imagination. She is now more fowl than human.

The completion of moral compensation, and with it the triumph of truth over beauty, has been witnessed by the disinterested gods and angels above.

Browning's film had an extensive degree of censorship, including a legal ban in England lasting thirty years, until 1963—a badge of cult honor for many.[3] Again, the graphic issue of disfigured and mutated bodies was the primary cause of *Freaks'* distribution problems. Celebrated 1960s photographer Diane Arbus devoted much of her black and white work to the hidden world of physical freaks. Arbus, like Browning before her, received unkind judgments by various critics for exploiting the lives of such misfortunate individuals. What these critics seemed to miss was the special trust given to Browning and Arbus in order to render so many unguarded, intimate scenes before the camera. Equally curious to Browning fans is the sly treatment of sexual games, gossip, and arousal within these carnival strata. In *Freaks*, a Siamese twin is kissed and her sister reacts to the pleasurable sensation. When the troupe members visit the newborn of the bearded lady, Phroso the clown remarks: "Ain't it cute. What is it?" Romance and flirtation are evidently on the minds of many of the story's characters and they proceed freely with such feelings. It is as if our lust and private behavior can be seen magnified within the fun house mirror of Madame Tetralini's circus.

Freaks employs a lengthy prologue instructing the viewer how the film should be perceived. It briefly mentions the long mistreatment of people born with extreme abnormalities and why this film intends to present another side to society's cruel stigmatizing. There is no intended irony to the didacticism or the narrative melodrama that makes this film even more of an archeological document. Apparently, in early work prints of Browning's film, the chase leading to Hercules' capture suggested that the freaks had castrated him before the murder.[4] Images from Browning haunt: a limbless torso lights and smokes a cigarette, pinheads dance in a pastoral meadow, actor Johnny Eck on two hands runs and spins without legs—one cannot think of a more disturbing motion picture from this decade.

Tod Browning went on to direct three more movies before ending his career in 1939. One can speculate as to the motives for this abrupt and early retirement. Browning might have lost his will and his appetite to forge on with his brand of narrative. Fashion and story were transforming significantly into the next decade of movie-making. Horror films were no longer in vogue and studio funding became exceedingly difficult to obtain. Furthermore, World War II was unleashing its hell on three continents.

King Kong (1933)

Because *King Kong* remains proudly secure in our lexicon and resonates so ubiquitously throughout both popular and high intellectual strata, proffering one of the most recognizable icons in fur, this extraordinary film—like its outsized, primate star—has been analyzed, discussed, and stalked to death. But to sidestep this 1933 title would be akin to ignoring the 900-pound gorilla in one's living room. *King Kong* casts a giant shadow of awe, fear and delight. The very life and soul of this movie speaks of the Great Depression. We need not see despondent soup lines and tenement squalor to establish the difficult era; the period announces itself through a very exotic escapism from our jobless, pandemic urban hunger.

King Kong is an imposing force of nature—a god among animals—brought in chains against his will from the deepest jungle to New York. Keeping in mind the many Tarzan tales, prevalent in print and on film, sound a similar chord of contrasting intelligent apes against human endeavors. But in this titanic story of Kong, the unyielding matinee idol is both prehistoric monster and a courageous classic hero of surprising complexity, emotion, and defiance. Moreover, cautious dialectic exists in viewing Kong as a political metaphor of the 1930s. If the giant ape represents the unrestrained menace of economic pain and misfortune run amok upon the broad populace, then there is a knowable victory once Kong falls from the Empire State building. Such an action is akin to slaying the Sphinx and freeing ancient Thebes of its plague. But if we reverse the identification and make Kong the consummate victim of our collective fears, then the film's conclusion is deeply sorrowful. Kong as the noble, sympathetic hero has considerable play for both cult and mainstream audiences.

The further we move from the historic Depression, the more we perceive Kong as an archetypal folk hero. Kong as a fearless and spirited combatant, who was abducted from his sheltered homeland where he reigned supreme, has to contend with the idiocy of cheap theatre vaudeville leading to the fatal aerial attack over Manhattan. Audiences from all epochs may think King Kong forbidding, but support swings around to him in the film's final reels. Kong's profound gentleness with Ann (legendary Fay Wray) and how he removes her from harm's way mitigates his unchecked violence in the city. With Kong's death the movie sounds a thundering note of tragedy.

The operative words governing *King Kong* must be transgression and exploitation. The film begins with an innocent manuever by documentary sensationalist Carl Denham, searching for a fresh feminine face from the hard streets of a depressed New York to star in his next film. He finds Ann Darrow—unemployed—who has no other choice but to join him. On their ship to remote Skull Island, Carl and Ann become intimate. How can it be any other way? Transgression and exploitation occur again when the natives of the island kidnap Ann for their ritualistic sacrifices to a god called Kong.

Other significant and more obvious metaphors can be discerned in the story. Kong might be seen as a stand-in for a proud, Southern black man who suffers unrelenting bias and destruction in a Northern city. Taking this analogy further, we can examine the deep-seated xenophobia of a homogenous community toward the more powerful alien. Worse, *King Kong* strips away the racial fears of having a black man emerge with a beautiful blonde helpless in his arms. A similar racial theme set in 1930s Chicago was delineated in Richard Wright's esteemed novel, *Native Son* (1940).

From another angle, Kong transgresses when he escapes with Ann as his chosen bride to his ideal habitat. The decisive action serves a poetic miscegenation and a resounding taboo to Carl, Carl's crew, and the movie audience. Carl eventually frees Ann from Kong's control, although he loses several men in the endeavor. Once Carl's crew incapacitates Kong with gas bombs, Carl is inspired to exploit Kong as a quintessential novelty act in New York. Breaking away from the stage and the offending camera flashing paparazzi, Kong steals off again with Ann—now in her native land. Perhaps it was the undignified exhibition of Kong's bondage that underscores the worst transgression before he is slaughtered.

If there is a pronounced dichotomy within Carl Denham, the ironic episodic events involving his newly found love betrays his psychic dilemma. Here is a worldly man who is woefully negligent with a young, vulnerable woman in Kong's dangerous reach. We watch this aboard the ship—the Venture—*vis-à-vis* the natives, and on Scull Island, and most notably on a theatre stage in New York for all society to see. Yet, the film strongly defines Carl's love for Ann and we believe this love to be true. Carl's lesson of love and responsibility is paid for dearly.

King Kong was originally budgeted at $500,000 which in its day struck the film industry as rather lavish and questionable even for top tier projects.[5] The investment proved well worth the effort since the movie was a huge success for RKO and producer David O. Selznick. Co-directors Merian C. Cooper and Ernest B. Schoedsack began collaboration several years earlier with natural, exotic locales in Persia (Iran) and Siam (Thailand).[6] Their foreign travels prepared them for a work as complex as *King Kong* and they were supported by a talented team of collaborators: the magical proficiency of special effects director Willis O'Brien, the sophisticated and intricate score by composer Max Steiner, the seamless art of cinematographers Edward Linden, Vernon L. Walker, and J.O. Taylor.

This film stands as an absolute measure of all subsequent horror-fantasy films. *King Kong* illustrates an adapted fairy tale revision of "beauty and the beast." Yet in this version, a haunting virtue is bestowed upon both the beast and beauty despite the sustained sexual undertow. In 1982, Steven Spielberg's *E.T.* recycles quite a bit from Kong's story, minus the subconscious terrors of intimacy with a creature. Unlike Kong, the E.T. character subverts the psychological problem of "beauty and the beast" due to E.T.'s calculated charisma and harmless "canine" demeanor of *Lassie* (film debut, 1943). However, were we to cross-breed E.T. with the uncompromising sea monster in Spielberg's earlier *Jaws* (1975), we would more closely approximate the stature of Kong's manifest destiny. It is interesting to note, too, that the exceptional illusions found in the film brought New Zealand director Peter Jackson early in his career to discover the possibilities of stop-motion animation.[7]

In short, *King Kong* commands the most unique place in our cinematic imagination. This point has to be stressed doubly after the annihilation of the World Trade Towers (the 1982 remake featured the Trade Center) and Peter Jackson's latest 2006 extravaganza in which the audience is invited to accept Kong as Ann's rightful lover. Still, the original black and white Kong lives on forever atop the cherished Empire State Building, frozen in time, in a final act of magnificent rebellion against visceral fears of propeller pilots and the pitiful magnitudes below.

Reefer Madness (1936)

In 1936 Motion Pictures Ventures released a G & H Production entitled *Reefer Madness*. The sixty-seven minute gem was also known at various times in its distribution as *Doped Youth*, *The Burning Question*, *Tell Your Children*, and *Love Madness*. The safest thing to say about this inane quasi-documentary is how brilliant comedy can arise inadvertently from professional film ineptitude and insincere exploitation. The film, directed by Louise Gasnier and written by Arthur Hoerl, is a repository of didactic, outrageous falsehoods about the recreational drug marijuana and the undocumented allegations that cannabis leads to violent crime, sexual recklessness, and madness. The film was resurrected decades later by Keith Stroup, leader of National Organization for the Reform of Marijuana Laws (NORML). Stroup made his lucky find in the Library of Congress film archive and purchased a print for under $300, thanks to public domain laws. Debuting as a benefit event in 1972 at Manhattan's St. Marks cinema, *Reefer Madness* took on new cultural meaning.[8]

In its era, *Reefer Madness* was expected to instruct civic bodies such as the PTA and religious groups about the epidemic horror to come. Instead, the film found a far greater, more appreciative audience among college campuses and midnight movie palaces beginning in the early 1970s. And until the complete prohibition of tobacco smoking in American theatres (circa 1984), cult art and cinema houses gingerly looked the other way when *Reefer Madness* audiences lit up in the upstairs smoking balconies. Infrequently, the police would bust these lenient theatres.

The unspoken indictment in this story suggests that the white middle class communities and their precious teenage youths were vulnerable to the satanic temptations of jazz and other uncontrollable vices throbbing seductively in black urban communities. The very term, "reefer," comes directly from black jazz circles of the 1920s and 1930s. White America was indeed frightened by the music, the language, the sexuality, and the drugs emanating from the exotic inner city world of black Americans. Happily, the obvious ironies about drugs and other counterculture pleasures in America, which surround *Reefer Madness*, reach Olympian heights and echo today's suburban fears about gangsta rap and black chic.

The cautionary film starts with a stiffly delivered prologue from "Dr. Carroll" about the spreading blight he calls marijuana addiction. The tale involves the reprehensible Mae Coleman and her partner in crime, Jack. Like a spider wearing a cool Stetson hat, Jack brings unsuspecting high school students to Mae's apartment, where their prey partake in manic marijuana parties (her fictional name most likely inspired by Hollywood's amoral diva—Mae West). These shady gatherings are populated by attractive, clean-cut high schoolers—

young men in neat jackets and ties, and young ladies in proper wool knits who listen spellbound to a white, intoxicated jazz pianist hitting the keys faster than the Road Runner.

We follow a model high school couple, Mary and Bill, who become entangled in Jack and Mae's web of iniquity through the devious efforts of a mutual pal, Jimmy. Regrettably, every circle of friends has a "Jimmy." Upon smoking one joint, poor Bill is undone and lost forever. He finds himself spending the night with Blanche in Mae's bedroom. Sadly, Mary hunts her boyfriend to Mae's abode. Within minutes, Mary falls prey to the bewitching drug. The party gets wilder; Mary is shot dead in a tragic error. Bill has passed out in a daze. When he awakes, Jack and Mae convince Bill that he killed his beloved Mary. Due to the marijuana, Bill has no memory of anything. Consequently, Bill goes to trial. All the while, two other school chums—Ralph and Blanche—know what really happened but they feel compromised by their vast marijuana consumption that fateful night.

The subplot has Jack trying to murder Ralph in order to keep the truth from the authorities. This eventually backfires and Jack is killed instead. Bill is found guilty in court. But in a stunning reversal, Mae and Blanche clue in the police and the conviction is thrown out. Ralph never recovers from his marijuana insanity or his mad eye twitch. Blanche commits suicide. Bill, ever the wiser, frees himself from cannabis forever. The film concludes with a stirring sermon from "Dr. Carroll."

The unreality of this movie is altogether astounding. Despite all the serious smoking on screen, no actor actually manages to inhale. To the viewer, the charming *Reefer Madness* characters just puff away like kids blowing bubbles at Chuck E. Cheese. One is reminded of President Bill Clinton's notorious disclaimer of trying grass in England but never inhaling. Further, the utter whiteness and conformity of the ensemble adds to the social surrealism. Certainly, there were people of color at Mae's caught in this awful drug vortex, if history has any accuracy. One also must question the respectable clothing depicted as though these characters were at church. But of most fascination is the movie's rendering of grass's violent influence, its terrible speed-like effects on to all body movement, and the drug's ability to bring instant insanity with the first toke. A sinister observation: neither Mae nor Jack smokes. No, they prefer alcohol. Mae and Jack stay cool and in control. However, national medical studies today would vilify alcohol, and not marijuana, as the supreme antisocial drug that causes unchecked violence and mental illness. In its inauthentic reportage, debauched moralizing, and hokey melodrama, *Reefer Madness* is truly a perverse fairy tale "flashing" its sex and drugs. The title joins ranks with other like-minded period films such as and the tawdry anti-VD films force-fed to the American military. Cult films author Danny Peary recalls an anti-syphilis film that portrayed soldiers entertaining a beautiful woman who in turn infects them. The military stopped presenting the movie after hearing the men argue that she was certainly worth the pain.[9]

Reefer Madness, one of the clumsiest and dumbest films ever made, attempts to portray American lost innocence, but paradoxically the filmmakers appear wonderfully naïve and moronic to all generations. In its painfully pathetic faux-documentary trappings, the film inadvertently pioneered the more polished fake documentaries to come such as *Spinal Tap* (1984), *Prêt-A-Porter* (1994), and *Best In Show* (2000).

Notes:

1.   John H. Richards, *In the Little World: A True Story of Dwarfs, Love and Trouble* (New York: HarperCollins, 2001), 3.

2.   Danny Peary, *Cult Movies* (New York: Dell, 1981), 107.

3.   Peary, *Cult Movies*, 109.

4.   Karl French and Philip French, *Cult Movies* (New York: Billboard Books, 2000), 98.

5.   Ray Morton, *King Kong: The History of a Movie Icon from Fay Wray to Peter Jackson* (New York: Applause Books, 2005), 29.

6.   Morton, *King Kong: The History of a Movie Icon from Fay Wray to Peter Jackson*, 8.

7.   Morton, *King Kong: The History of a Movie Icon from Fay Wray to Peter Jackson*, 56.

8.   J. Hoberman and Jonathan Rosenbaum, *Midnight Movies* (New York: Da Capo Press, 1983), 262.

9.   Danny Peary, *Cult Movies* (New York: Dell, 1981), 293.

Chapter Three
Films from the 1940s

The face of Western Civilization was transfigured by the violent upheavals during World War II and the terrifying Holocaust. Approximately six million Jews were slaughtered in Europe and over sixteen million soldiers were either killed or left missing in action. Never has the world witnessed this much carnage. European intellectuals and artists in staggering numbers fled Hitler, creating a new wave of thinking, art, design, and culture on American shores. Abstract Expressionism was the exciting new visual concept in galleries and museums as the center of art shifted from Paris to New York. The previous American isolationism vanished the day Japan bombed Pearl Harbor. The overwhelming unemployment problem from the previous decade was curiously solved during wartime thanks to general conscription of all able-bodied men and the shift to hyper-drive in American factories. President Franklin Roosevelt died in office April 1945 and our nation celebrated victory in the European theatre presided over by President Harry Truman on May 8, 1945. To his credit, Truman had ordered the full integration of white and black men within the uniformed services. The Nuclear Age began with the atomic bombing of two Japanese cities Hiroshima and Nagasaki. As many social philosophers and essayists have proclaimed in the chilliest of tones, "the nuclear genie is out of the bottle."

America assumed the role of a global superpower rivaled only by its war ally Russia, led by Josef Stalin. Stalin moved to dominate much of Eastern Europe as part of the negotiated post-war agreement with Truman and England's Churchill. This sowed the seeds of the Cold War that would last for decades to come. The primal fear of Communism began in the late 1940s and would emerge like a political plague in the early 1950s. The United States initiated the encompassing Marshall Plan, giving aid to so many broken European countries. Regrettably, the United States began to understand the enormity of the Holocaust only as the postwar years unfolded, and not earlier. The baby boom phenomenon began with the sweeping influx of returning soldiers from Europe and the Pacific campaigns. The GI Bill of Rights created a compelling opportunity for young veterans to continue their higher education, changing forever the notion that college was an elite privilege.

In 1941, penicillin became a practical medicine that revolutionized healthcare and was a sizable redress to venereal disease. One of the first computers, ENIAC, standing two stories tall and weighing 60,000 pounds, came into being in 1945. In music composition, there was a new thrust toward classical dissonance, spearheaded by European refugees Arnold Schoenberg, Paul Hindemith, and Béla Bartók. Big bands led by Duke Ellington, Glenn Miller, and Tommy Dorsey still dominated radio and live performance. Bebop, jazz, and rhythm and blues were offshoots of the big band sound as highlighted by Thelonious Monk, Ella Fitzgerald, and Woody Herman.

Contributing to the literature of the period were Norman Mailer, Shirley Jackson, Tennessee Williams, Arthur Miller, William Saroyan, and Langston Hughes. The decade supported a gigantic growth of commercial films, with many titles and stories aimed toward Americans during wartime. From *Casablanca* (1942) to *The Best Years of Our Lives* (1946), Hollywood kept offering morally uncomplicated plots that separated good from evil and vilified all Germans and Japanese. Orson Welles' masterpiece *Citizen Kane* (1941) maintained a position quite outside the major studio output and the uncompromising film earned the wrath of newspaper titan William Randolph Hearst, who was the undisguised target of Welles' caustic tale. Walt Disney built a formidable empire with high quality, ambitious animated features such as *Fantasia* (1940). In the midst of the war years, Disney fashioned cartoons for the government, such *Donald Gets Drafted* and *Der Fuehrer's Face*.

Commercial television became viable in the late 1940s with over a dozen public stations serving parts of the nation. The first sitcom debuted January 1949—*The Goldberg*, which originated from radio broadcasts. At the end of World War II there were just 5,000 television sets. Six years later, 17 million sets had been purchased. *Kukla, Fran & Ollie* was the first children's show on the tube in 1947.

I Walked with a Zombie (1943)

Admittedly, the film's lurid title conjures the worst associations, but many film historians have found a wealth of subtlety, mysticism, and melancholy in the 1943 RKO Radio/Val Lewton production *I Walked with a Zombie*. The film, directed by Frenchman Jacques Tourneur, was based on Inez Wallace's story of the same title from a Hearst Sunday newspaper magazine.[1] Wallace's tale centered on the slow moving, unnatural beings whom she had encountered on a Haitian farm. She had claimed that these very present creatures were not dead, yet their vocal chords and their free will were ripped away by an unknown poison. Wallace went to Haiti a skeptic and came back a devout believer in the supernatural island arts. To the author, these soulless individuals acted like indentured slaves performing menial tasks on the grounds. Both Wallace's story and director Jacques Tourneur's film wisely avoid the most sensational aspects of voodoo and third world exotica. The film's undeniable power comes from Tourneur's knowledge of the senses in creating textured atmosphere, painterly shadows, and hyper-rhythmic percussion. Put simply, the film makes a convincing case for the acceptance of zombie existence and the hidden realms of purgatory on earth.

I Walked with a Zombie invariably falls under the horror film category and was produced with that genre in mind. However, within the sophisticated narrative action there is very little of the standard horror machinery to startle us. The film's plotline has an American nurse assigned to Paul Holland's island homestead. The nurse, played vulnerably by Frances Dee, soon discovers that her charge, Holland's wife Jessica, is not ill in the conventional sense. Holland is certain that Jessica has gone mad and he feels responsible for her precipitous. Yet the Haitians believe something quite different. Holland's brother Wesley longs for Jessica but cannot act on his suppressed desires. Holland and his nurse find a deepening emotional intimacy tempting them to imagine what life would be like without Jessica. Even shock therapy fails and Jessica is escorted to a voodoo ceremony. The potent native drums provide the final thrust toward Jessica's deliverance. Tragically, Wesley is driven to stab his beloved and follows her into the sea.

The film's premise may impress some viewers as *Jane Eyre* in the Caribbean and, indeed, producer Val Lewton had joked to his colleague that modeling the Bronte work was distinctly his intention.[2] Examining *Jane Eyre's* romantic intrigue from a fresh, folkloric perspective, Jessica's insanity and catatonia has metaphoric intensity. One may interpret the sins and the ills of colonialism as the unspoken justification for Jessica's desultory state. Even more curious is the fact that if Jessica's pain and punishment are deliberate, eternal, and absolute, why is her husband spared a greater suffering? After all, he is the plantation owner and the standard bearer for all colonialists. Stated bluntly, why is Holland allowed to have a second chance at happiness with the young beautiful nurse? The film does not answer this question. Further, there remains an uncomfortable impasse between familiar Christianity and Haitian native religion.

Director Tourneur leans delicately toward respecting the misunderstood and maligned culture of voodoo and the unsettling magic of the West Indies. The film utilizes a few presentational tactics such as a Calypso troubadour in a choral counterpoint to the story's action and a spare voiceover narration. Further, Tourneur's relies heavily on the weight and tension of sustained silences that help deliver the film's unique spell. The original score is by Roy Webb and the general quality of his composition is more layered and atmospheric than narrative-based program music. Once the pounding drums begin in the distance, a secret world rises from the ashen earth. Equally skillful is cinematographer J. Roy Hunt's chiaroscuro handling of light and shadow in stillness and in rapid motion. Several key scenes are shot in extreme darkness; when the nurse's first encounter with Jessica on the winding descent of what at first appears to be a sepulchral staircase of stone is a striking example. Another beautifully haunting shot occurs in the nurse's bedroom with a larger than life silhouette floating across wrought iron swirling circles and bars.

Tourneur's father Maurice was a highly regarded silent film director who brought to his work similar visual elements of strong, angular light and shadow, with surprising emotional scale, to his story's canvases. One can only assume that Jacques Tourneur built intelligently on the foundation of his father. Jacques Tourneur preceded *I Walked with a Zombie* with another favorite cult film, *Cat People* (1942). His other highly regarded titles include *Out of the Past* (1947), *The Body Snatcher* (1945), and *The Leopard Man* (1943). *I Walked with a Zombie* was one of three Lewton/Tourneur collaborations centering on an average protagonist caught up in doubt and moral complexity engaged by foreign culture.[3]

Prominent 1940s film critic James Agee commended Tourneur's work in several Lewton films and Agee appraised actress Francis Dee in glowing terms: "One of the very few women in movies who really had a face . . . and always used this translucent face with deliberate and exciting talent."

Tourneur, who died in 1977, found Hollywood a sensible and viable home for nearly thirty years. His career was solid and steady, yet decidedly underappreciated given his range of talent. He was honored posthumously by the The Film Society of Lincoln Center in its 2002 series, "Whispers in a Distant Corridor: The Cinema of Jacques Tourneur."

Dead of Night (1945)

As a mid-century study in metaphysical terror, the classic British ghost film, *Dead of Night* (1945), must receive qualified high praise, in part due to the unusual collaborative nature of the film team and the subtle unevenness in tone and spirit of the partitioned tales. Despite this minor reservation, the film is frequently considered the most accomplished horror compilation that appeals paradoxically to the rationalist, the agnostic, and the supernatural believer. Mid-century American horror writer/producer Milton Subotsky called the film, "the greatest horror film ever."[4]

The 1945 film from Ealing Studios was written by Angus Macphail who was one of Alfred Hitchcock's close friends and who provided Hitchcock with the "MacGuffin device" in storyboarding ("MacGuffin" is usually the missing object that is part of the crime plotting).[5] There are four credited directors—Alberto Calvalcanti, Charles Chrichton, Basil Dearden, and Robert Hamer—who were parceled out a section east in the form of a digest, that tie together in the end ingeniously. The whirlwind finale, lasting around four minutes, has the spirit, velocity, and articulate madness of the best LSD trips—and may spare the viewer any flashbacks. Helping to unify the segments, the renowned French artist Georges Auric composed the film score. To the casual viewer, then and now, *Dead of Night* should seem quite whole and consistent; for this feat, the producer must be credited. The essential concept to the story concerns the eerie feeling of *déjà vu* and the undisclosed ramifications of the phenomenon. The film's framing device is rather bald but effective: at a remote country home an assembly discusses the accident of an uninvited guest. Conversation veers immediately to the subject of disturbing dreams and inner motivations.

One can detect a traceable whiff of playwright Luigi Pirandello's double reality fanaticism within the film. Although this is not exactly Pirandello's *Six Characters In Search of an Author*, *Dead of Night* might be subtitled "Six Dreamers in Search of a Victim." The central character, an anxious Kafkaesque architect, is convinced that the other guests are featured in his recurring nightmare. The architect's complaint on surface seems solipsistic. Several guests recount private ghost stories from past experience. Eventually the film's energies coalesce in an electrifying climax.

Horror anthologies have never been a successful genre. If one story lacks integrity, the entire omnibus fails. Another common problem can be found in the bond that unifies the contributing tales. Occasionally applauded efforts, such as the grotesque *Creepshow* (1982), lack the pathological expressiveness of *Dead of Night*. More prevalent are mediocre examples: *Dr. Terror's House of Horrors* (1964), *Night Gallery* (1969), *Twilight Zone* (1983), and *Cat's Eye* (1985).

The episodic structure of *Dead of Night* is both practical and deceptively simple, custom tailored to actor Mervyn Johns' understated, frightened profile of Craig. Craig anticipates certain events that eventually come true. The ensemble acts out, or reenacts—depending on the final analysis—a series of casual actions. The resident doctor explains each incident in empirical, rational terms. True to Freudian interpretation of waking dreams and hallucinations, Craig's recurring dream is maddeningly hazy and incomplete. To some of the story's characters, what is discussed has no more threat than the average ghostly parlor game among friends. The film situates the action among the ostensible strangers is charming, familiar, safe, and disarming. Because mischief is in the air, the collective aim, at the start, seems to rebut the sustained scientific skepticism of the token psychiatrist, Dr. van Straaten.

There is a method behind the stacking order of the vignettes that probably is better appreciated intuitively than from a blackboard analysis. Remotely, Italo Calvino's mysterious novel, *Castle of Crossed Destinies* (1969), uses a similar contrivance in the grouping of strangers inside an atmospheric shelter, but for Calvino, the social dialogue can occur only through the device of "divination" tarot cards. Calvino's characters, for some unexplained reason, are struck dumb at the start of his story. Of course, bundling strangers within a fortified rural home is a well-celebrated convention in the works of Agatha Christie and other mystery writers.

The first two tightly crafted tales feature novel twists and are sustained by their respective brevity. A race car driver, Hugh, has a nightmare about a phantom hearse and the jolly, yet mordant invitation, "Just room for one more, sir!" Those very words are spoken again by a bus driver and the premonition kept Hugh from boarding the bus and being killed. A woman recalls playing hide-and-seek with a troubled little boy during a Christmas party at a country house. The crying child apparently was the ghost of a boy murdered years ago by a malicious sister. The impressive third tale, "Haunted Mirror," explores a magic looking-glass that mirrors its own tragic past. The common, primitive fear about mirrors and cameras resonates within this vignette. A woman describes her Victorian mirror gift to her fiancé, but he sees the image of a chamber that is the scene of a spousal murder. Director Robert Hamer made his professional debut with this piece and his work demonstrated proficiency in complex camera angles that intimate eerie and maddening ambiguities.

What follows is the thinnest dramatic offering, "Golfing Story," involving a ghoulish wager between golfers that ends in farcical death. Two sportsmen—played by the famed British comic duo Naunton Wayne and Basil Radford—

argue over love and play out 18 holes to discern who will win the woman of their dreams. However, the cheating winner is haunted by the loser. Perhaps the defense for this segment was to add comic relief to leaven the other morbid material.

Suffice it to say, that final glorious vignette by Michael Cavalcanti, that depicts a tormented ventriloquist and his rebellious dummy sounds a subversive note of perverse genius. Cavlacanti, a Brazilian of modest cinematic achievement, had a serious background in art and architecture; he worked on the avant-garde classic *L'Inhumaine* (1924). "The Ventriloquist's Dummy" serves as the chief justification to highlight *Dead of Night* in this cult study. No other 1940s film can match Cavalcanti's sly, uncompromising execution of a theatrical psyche in existential throes. Actor Michael Redgrave's total and unguarded commitment to his role as the ventriloquist is one of the reasons the dramatic surprises function so exceptionally. His character is stripped bare by his aggressive, sadistic dummy Hugo. To add to the ventriloquist's misery, Hugo has signaled his desire to leave "the act" in order partner with another ventriloquist. The turning point within the vignette occurs when Hugo is found like an unfaithful lover in the rival's hotel suite. Clearly, this vignette's wicked treatment of a severely damaged split personality has spawned similar horror films such as *Psycho* (1960), *Magic* (1978), and *Child's Play* (1988), and the British play *Comedians* (1975), which subsequently became a BBC film. One can also draw a direct psychic tie from Michael Redgrave's keen portrayal to Anthony Perkins' masterful Norman Bates in *Psycho*. Curiously enough, *Dead of Night* went into production before the end of the war yet the tone of the film has no bearing on that reality.[6] One might assume that the entire film was a ghost from an earlier decade when all was idyllic beyond the walls of the country estate.

Beauty and the Beast / La Belle et la Bête (1946)

Jean Cocteau's film output was slender in the best sense; as an artist he expressed his dreamlike visions in ways that amused, enchanted, and exposed Jean Cocteau—through poems, plays, canvases and books. What defines Cocteau uniquely, what charmed his public, what mesmerized his critics was his inner dance of innocence, surrealistic whimsy, and refined cynicism. As explained in his memoirs, he viewed himself first and foremost a poet, neither a cold thinker nor a stolid philosopher, and his *Beauty and the Beast* (La Belle et la Bête) has endured as a pure and profound fairy tale for all ages and eras. Further, the exotic enchantment of the story propelled him to state, "That is why I care to live just as much in Beauty's family as in the Beast's castle."[7]

Cocteau came to cinema when he turned forty with his influential short film *The Blood of a Poet* (1930). He was assisted by the same patron, Vicomte de Noailles, who helped Buñuel and Dalí make their second collaborative film, *L'Âge d'Or* (1930). Cocteau's first film, tied to the Orphic theme, was full of self-absorption and, in the main, a meditation on death's proximity toward creativity. During the German occupation, Cocteau wrote for other filmmakers but resisted making another film until after the war when he decided to go ahead with a retelling of Madame Leprince de Beaumont's 18th century classic, *Beauty and the Beast*.

Cocteau was prudent in his choice to employ another confident French director René Clément as his special effects consultant. Cinematographer Henri Alekan was responsible for the impressive modulation between natural exterior shots and exquisite interior fantasies. Cocteau enlisted the brilliant Christian Bérard to supervise all areas of makeup, costumes, and stage sets.[8] The stated goal was to render "realism of the unreal." The costumes proved to be terribly challenging to the cast—namely, the Beast's preparation time lasting over five hours each day, the unbearable heat and discomfort, and the degree of trial and error with each design. The pains and mistakes were well worth it for the sum of the parts proved to be nearly perfect. This film is thoroughly gorgeous to the eye and the mind.

One helpful avenue to assess the enchantment and singularity of Cocteau's first film would be by way of Disney Studios. In the late 1930s and early 1940s, Walt Disney's animators pioneered adroit full length features of *Snow White*, *Pinocchio*, and *Dumbo*. These animations were ingenious, graceful amalgams of cute action animals and storybook characters, often embracing musical theatre routines and vaudevillian comedy. To Disney's credit, the overall look was smartly standardized, commercially broad, yet artistically exceptional.

Walt Disney seemed to have his hand on the public's pulse despite the fact that Disney never left, as it were, a single fingerprint on his body of work. Cocteau, by contrast, focused solely on his pedigree sensibility and the deeper recesses of the unconscious mind. Of course, one also senses the influential cultural distinctions between French and American storytelling within these two film artists. Gallic and European heritage filters throughout Cocteau's imagination, whereas Disney appropriates at will from several nations and treasure chests. Cocteau's *Beauty and the Beast* feels composed for older children and for those adults who can reawaken their lost childhoods in secret and in twilight. Most Disney films seem to ask the adult viewers to do the same in public under far safer light, and in the presence of their own children. Disney's creative dependency on popular song, dance, and total musical engagement denotes a major divergence from Cocteau's cinematic canvases.

Furthermore, Disney staked out wholly new territory for family viewing while astutely managing the bludgeoning economics of expensive studio animation. Cocteau's interpretation of *Beauty and the Beast* was piercingly personal and troubling, employing uncanny camera tricks and intuitively simpler effects. It would be impossible to associate a large consortium of artists and artisans such as Disney Studios with the making of Cocteau's masterpiece. Yet, both Jean Cocteau and Walt Disney were highly motivated to explore and revitalize children's fantasy without imposing elitist filters. For Cocteau this goal was even more significant after the sustained suffering and slaughter from a world war. For Disney, this was his personal calling and a lifetime industry through the Great Depression, World War II, and the longer respite of peacetime.

As is very well known, the Disney Studios animated treatment of *Beauty and the Beast* finally arrived forty-five years after the French version. Many of the narrative elements remain the same, but the tone and timber of the fairy tale had converted to something thoroughly unrelated to Cocteau and European fables. Cocteau realized his film during the height of Freud's influence, essentially positioning a fable's inventiveness within the hybrid of surrealism and psychoanalytic counterpoint. For example, the Beast's home was designed to maximize the fantastical opulence of Spanish artists such as Salvador Dalí and Antonio Gaudí. Statues move in the manner of powdered mimes in a Paris street. Smoke circulates magically from the Beast's fingers. Some of this is utterly playful, while other illusory conceits are disconcerting and neurotic in the best application. There is a discernible concept of dread and calm horror within every scene inside this lost country estate. Disney's animated objects within *Beauty and the Beast* appear factory fresh, safe, pre-tested, and ready for licensing by Mattel, Hasbro, and other toy makers. To defend the Disney treatment, it should be noted that esteemed critic James Agee, with reserved judgment, was not exactly overwhelmed by Cocteau's accomplishment, "Cocteau's *Beauty and the Beast* seems to me no sort of miracle, but it is a thoroughly satisfying movie."[9]

Cocteau stayed close to the celebrated fairy tale. He had identified the story as British in origin and he credited Madame Leprince de Beaumont (1711-1780) for gathering supernatural castle myths from England and Scotland.[10] Taboos of the original story are maintained. Cocteau's Beauty lives with her father in a spacious rural home. There is no mother. Her sisters avoid household work, putting the burden on Beauty. In that one respect the story has an early parallel to *Cinderella*. Beauty's brother also has undesirable features and lacks virtue. Beauty is drawn to her brother's attractive friend, Avenant. When Beauty's father visits the city he learns that he is financially ruined—seemingly his first dramatic mistake. Returning home, he loses himself in the woods. Thickets and hedges separate as if commanded, and Beauty's father stumbles into a decrepit estate. The next morning he takes a rose—his second mistake—from the castle grounds, which prompts a feral Beast in high baroque clothing to threaten the poor man with death for the theft of his cherished flower. Beauty's father convinces the Beast to delay his execution so that he can bid farewell to his family. In addition, the creature suggests to the old man that one of his daughters can be sacrificed to spare him. Beauty learns the awful news and finds her way to the Beast. Did Beauty instinctively know that she could undo the damage? When Beauty introduces herself to her father's predator, the Beast softens considerably. She stays in the castle and the Beast repeatedly entreats her to marry him.

Because her father has fallen sick, the Beast grants Beauty a brief leave. Back home, Beauty's tears turn into diamonds, tempting her sisters to concoct a scheme to send all the younger characters to the terrible castle. Beauty discovers that she is in love with the Beast, who is perishing from her unrequited love. Beauty's old flame, Avenant, is stung by a statue's magic arrow. Avenant morphs into the doomed creature of the estate just as the Beast dies in Beauty's loving embrace. The Beast now assumes the persona of the Prince—his true identity. Beauty and the Prince become airborne in their newly minted bliss.

Cocteau declared, "To fairlyland as people usually see it, I would bring a kind of realism to banish the vague and misty nonsense now so completely outworn." He went on to state in the same press release, "The poet Paul Eluard says that to understand my film version of *Beauty and the Beast* you must love your dog more than your car. Ordinarily, I would settle for that."[11] Obtaining some of the most basic supplies became a feat of magic as the production crew resorted to odd sources and the unseemly black market. Jean Marais performed three roles: the Beast, Avenant, and the Prince. Both Jean Marais and Cocteau's female lead, Mila Parély, were frequently ill. Moreover, Cocteau contracted jaundice in the making of this film. At the modest film premiere June 1, 1946, in the presence of colleagues and select guests, Cocteau was taken by great fear. Asked to greet the audience before the screening, Cocteau fell absolutely silent and he held Marlene Dietrich's hand for dear life during the 90-minute debut.[12] Speaking to the success of a subsequent Cocteau movie but obviously alluding to Cocteau's entire oeuvre, fellow director Henri-Georges Clouzot proclaimed, "that film proves that there's no such thing as technique, but only invention."

Notes:

1   Chris Fuiwara and Martin Scorsese, *Jacques Tourneur: The Cinema of Nightfall* (Baltimore: The Johns Hopkins University Press, 1998), 85.

2   Danny Peary, *Cult Movies* (New York: Dell, 1981), 150.

3   Chris Fuiwara and Martin Scorsese, *Jacques Tourneur: The Cinema of Nightfall* (Baltimore: The Johns Hopkins University Press, 1998), 6.

4   Peter Hutchings, *The Amicus House of Horror;* Steve Chibnall. Ed. *British Horror Cinema* (London and New York: Routledge, 2002), 136.

5   Karl French and Philip French, *Cult Movies* (New York: Billboard Books, 2000), 68.

6   French and French, *Cult Movies*, 68.

7   Jean Cocteau and Elizabeth Sprigge, trans., *The Difficulty of Being* (New York: Peter Owens Ltd and Editions du Rocher, 1967), 50.

8   Jean Cocteau and Ronald Duncan, trans., *Beauty and the Beast: Diary of a Film* (New York: Dover Publications. 1972), 6-7.

9   James Agee, *Agee on Film: Criticism and Comment on the Movies* (New York: McDowell, Oblensky, 1958), 286.

10   Jean Cocteau, Robert Phelps and Richard Howard, trans., *Professional Secrets, An Autobiography of Jean Cocteau* (New York, Evanston, San Francisco, London: Harper & Row, Publishers 1972), 195.

11   Jean Cocteau, *Once Upon A Time—French Poet Explains His Filming of Fairy Tale,* DVD liner notes (Criterion Collection, 1998).

12   Jean Cocteau, Robert Phelps and Richard Howard, trans., *Professional Secrets, An Autobiography of Jean Cocteau* (New York, Evanston, San Francisco, London: Harper & Row, Publishers 1972), 233-234.

Chapter Four
Films from the 1950s

A half century ago, the United States experienced a buoyant economic climb unseen in nearly three decades. Our nation was in ascendancy as a superpower and enjoyed the profound influence assisting the rebuilding of Europe after world war. The explosive growth of suburbia came about in part by the G.I. Bill, which rendered home ownership an affordable prospect even at the expense of the declining inner cities. The arms race between America and the Soviet Union intensified over the decade. With this cold hostility between two former World War II allies came a "Red Scare," enabled considerably by Senator Joe McCarthy from Wisconsin. The 1954 McCarthy Senate hearings seared the political soul of our society and increased the complexity of understanding Communism and the Communist threat to America. The immeasurable damage that stemmed from the Senate hearings filtered into many aspects of our nation's life and with the inconclusive 1953 ceasefire in the Korean War, arrested in part the political will of the Eisenhower White House. So much of this decade of ambiguity and conformity was in direct contrast to the 1940s, and yet critical milestones in civil rights took hold. The landmark 1954 Supreme Court Decision Brown v. Board of Education spun the country in a dramatic new direction with respect to public school integration and changing race relations. Likewise, Rosa Parks' historic act of civil disobedience on a bus ride in Montgomery, Alabama grabbed the nation's focus in 1955. Two years after Parks, Central High School in Little Rock was transformed permanently by nine black teenage students who dared to enter the all-white school. The Democratic party dominated the south and found its identity at odds with the impulsive, rebellious directions of North Carolina's influential Senator, Strom Thurmond.

Labor unions were still powerful elements in the United States and had influence in electoral politics. Manufacturing was a pronounced component of America's economic identity, and GM President Charles Erwin Wilson is famously misquoted from his Senate hearing to become Defense Secretary: "What's good for General Motors was good for the country." Television had infiltrated American homes in the manner of a consumer epidemic. Mr. Television—Milton Berle—and his *Texaco Star Theatre* endeared the comedian to homes across the land. Idealized family shows like *Leave it to Beaver* and *Ozzie and Harriet* cast a seamless hypnotic spell.

In American literature, the Beat movement took hold in sharp opposition to material values and economic vanities. William S. Burroughs' *Naked Lunch* and J. D. Salinger's *The Catcher in the Rye* captured much of the intellectually elite's mood about a nation in mothballs. Ralph Ellison's esteemed novel on race in America, *Invisible Man*, was a major statement at the heart of cultural identity. There was a sizable appetite for science fiction in literature and on screen. The first polio vaccine entered general use in 1955 and made Dr. Jonas Salk a world hero. When the Soviet Union launched Sputnik in 1957, America was more than unnerved by an enemy nation's bluster about interstellar domination.

The second half of the 1950s introduced Elvis Presley to the world. Along with Elvis came rock 'n roll and broadcasts of Dick Clark's *American Band Stand*. Jazz entered a new sophisticated phase with brilliant sounds from Miles Davis' "Birth of the Cool." Frank Sinatra had resurgence as a singer and a film actor. Hollywood premiered enduring films such as *On the Waterfront* (1954) and *Rebel without a Cause* (1955), crowning Marlon Brando and James Dean, respectively, as the decade's quintessential beautifully wounded icons of dimensionality and integrity. Director Alfred Hitchcock, relying on actor James Stewart, dominated the decade with a string of excellent suspense thrillers. Drive-in movie theatres sprouted in every region of the continent. Unrelated to that growth was the emergence of a prodigious interstate highway system, funded by congress to aid the evacuation of cities during nuclear attack. Along with fire drills, "duck and cover" exercises were the norm in most schools. Children crouched in fetal positions against the school's tile corridors as a "preventive measure" from an atomic blast. It was also an age of Silly Putty, hula hoops, and the birth of McDonald's hamburgers.

As a celebrated war general from the European theatre, President Eisenhower largely enjoyed a calming rapport with the country. His parting remarks to America about his reservations about the military-industrial complex are often cited as prescience of the highest magnitude.

Glen or Glenda (1952)

Michael Medved has "praised" Ed Wood, Jr. as the worst film director of all time, and the honorific resonates in so many directions.[1] The films of Ed Wood, Jr. have baffled a wide array of sophisticated observers of cinematic arts. Wood's idiocy and inanities as a low budget 1950s filmmaker were graced perchance by some hidden hand of God. This is a wild pronouncement, to be sure, but in the late 1980s and early 1990s a wave of enthusiasm and rediscovery hit the country, cresting with Tim Burton's homage to the late director, *Ed Wood* (1994).

Although Wood is most famous for using cheap flying saucer toys in his ludicrous *Plan Nine from Outer Space* (1959), his debut film *Glen or Glenda* presents a peculiar inner view of a vain man fighting, hiding, and celebrating his glorious love of wearing women's clothing. The film is wonderfully confessional and yet opaque in the revelation about self-definition and sexual tropes from the 1950s. There was no bold stroke of the imagination or compelling fantasy in creating *Plan Nine from Outer Space*, but madcap inspiration struck Wood with *Glen or Glenda*. *Plan Nine from Outer Space* trumpets a prolonged, bald note for world peace in the midst of our fear of Soviet Communist aggression. More practical in theme and content, *Glen or Glenda* examines why a man's head goes bald. The backdoor, campy appeal found within *Glen or Glenda* can be seen in Wood's cryptic, layering of richly insane, editorial narrative and self-serving, symbolic unreality that lacks any principle of unity. Over and over, Wood propounds an emotional plea to grant tolerance and social credit to the rights of transvestites while engaging functional delineations of American transsexual identity and homosexuality. Released during the height of the McCarthy anti-Communist witch hunts, Wood's rendering of secret identities in pain has genuine historic pathos. Knowing too that Dr. Alfred Kinsey was tracking in this decade the cavernous dark side of American sexuality, *Glen or Glenda* has legitimate psychological capacity to reach beyond Wood's fetishes and any pop autobiographical psychosis in the spirit of moral tolerance. Still, the film's inadvertent innocenct, self-catering transparencies cannot assist the viewer to a steady state of logic and film comprehension.

The fault does not lie with the editor, the cast, or the production budget. The overall product is so inescapably awful, and yet so personal to the filmmaker that some truthful, articulate madness guides each chaotic frame. The work assumes perfect form and offers a visual treatise of the most repressive of American decades. If investigative reporters, such as Anthony Summers, can claim that FBI czar J. Edgar Hoover was a cross-dresser and lover to his pal, Clyde Tolson, there should be a profound, unconscious thread to horror film legend, Bela Lugosi, narrating for Ed Wood.[2]

Viewing the film on face value, we experience the accommodations two divergent men make with their respective fates. Despite the film's ineptitude, a compelling struggle, depicting an individual resisting a repressed society, is diagrammed.[3] Outside the presentational framework sits Bela Lugosi. His character, either content or mildly sedated, accepts solitude inside his dimly lit, macabre laboratory. "Bevare, bevare!!" With a heavy Hungarian dialect, Lugosi addresses "startling things." No one watching—not even Lugosi—has a clue to what is being referenced. Someone has committed suicide after an arrest in public for cross-dressing. The police detective consults with a loquacious psychiatrist to comprehend the nature of these fascinating cross-dressers. The doctor explains that the condition is far more prevalent in society than we realize and yet there is no harm to anymore. He goes on to cover two clinical case histories, Glen and Alan. Without reasoning, we hear from Lugosi again that "their stories must be told!" The imperative ritual for the legendary Lugosi of enacting the stories has an air of some sacred annual observance like Easter or Passover.

Lugosi warns us to beware the dragon who likes to eat boys and fat snails, "snips and snails and puppy dog tails." His admonition is oddly comforting if for no other reason than Lugosi sounds like the Transylvanian Mr. Rogers. Many reports claim that Wood employed Lugosi for his deeply faded star power and Wood simply contrived for the legendary actor an inorganic and ludicrous role.

Wood's banal script is redolent of the hoary lessons of a basic sex education primer. Glen is engaged to an attractive blonde named Barbara. He fears letting on to her about his lifelong habit of wearing women's clothes. To make matters worse, he has a powerful hankering for Barbara's delicate, white, angora sweater. Glen's friend cautions him about this secret and urges him to tell Barbara the full truth. Glen does and Barbara is stunned. Still, her love for him is great and she lends him the coveted sweater. Such conflict resolution could happen this smoothly only in the 1950s. The psychiatrist consults with them and guides the couple to transcend the identity of Glenda by reinforcing Barbara's attributes to Glen.

With respect to the second case history, the psychiatrist describes Alan's condition as wholly unlike Glen's. Alan desires to be a woman, and enjoys the costuming of a woman. Alan's alter ego is Ann. Wood's second character study references the matter of undeveloped female organs. According to the doctor, Alan is a pseudo-hermaphrodite. Since hormone therapy has marginal results for Alan, he undergoes a sex change operation and transforms into Ann. The psychiatrist has proved two critical points to the detective. One, society has greatly misunderstood middle class men who love wearing women's clothes. Two, Glen and Alan are strikingly distinct from each other and remedies for each man's personal happiness take different routes. Both men deserve tribute and tolerance from the world at large, according to Ed Wood. *Glen or Glenda* may be the first American film to use the word homosexuality.[4]

Paramount Pictures, in 1981, picked up on the renewed interest in *Plan Nine from Outer Space* and Ed Wood's name by marketing *Glen or Glenda* as the next classic cult sensation.[5] In many uncanny ways, there are persuasive links between the 1950s Wood and the 1970s John Waters. Regrettably, the Paramount campaign failed out of the gate days before April Fools, thanks to a hostile piece in *New York* magazine. The studio pulled the film from release.

Beyond Wood's autobiographical drives, probing the film's *raison d'être* would lead us to the highly publicized, transsexual surgery of Christine Jorgensen in 1952. The tabloid journalism covered Jorgensen's operation: *New York Daily News* featured the story on its front page under the headline "Ex-GI Becomes Blonde Beauty." Low rent Hollywood producer George Weiss took notice of the Jorgensen case and moved quickly to build a film trading on sensationalism and sexual curiosity.[6] Ed Wood's transvestism made him a perfect candidate for the job and he was given a start-up budget. Wood's next task was to convince Lugosi, in spite of Lugosi's age and addictions, to collaborate on *Glen or Glenda*. By many accounts, Lugosi had genuine fondness for Ed Wood. After Lugosi died in 1956, Wood's modest film career eventually collapsed.

An afterthought: a few months after the historic attack on Pearl Harbor, Wood joined the Marines. He freely claimed that he fought in the Battle of Guadalcanal while sporting a bra and panties under his uniform.

Invaders from Mars (1953)

There are three indispensable cult films at the height of the Cold War centering on extraterrestrial encounters with aliens disguised in human form—*It Came from Outer Space* (1953), *Invaders from Mars* (1953), and *Invasion of the Body*

Snatchers (1956). If the 1950s *zeitgeist* unveiled any unwarranted humor, one could cite Zsa Zsa Gabor's *Queen from Outer Space* (1958) for her altruistic role as an insurgent fighting for the right to love all the men on Venus. More telling politically, *It Came from Outer Space*, based on a respectable story by Ray Bradbury, had a benign interpretation of alien agenda, while the other two invader films declared deep pessimism and panic about interplanetary contact. After all, the cunning space creatures in the Bradbury story want only to continue their voyage after they repair their crashed vehicle. In light of the paranoia about Communist invasion and infiltration within our government, our schools, our hospitals, and in our houses of worship, the handling of space invaders presented a convenient metaphor for accepting America's xenophobia and our need to attack leftist members of our own society.

Although the well plotted and thoughtful *Invasion of the Body Snatchers* became a wider known film in the culture of cult, William Cameron Menzies' *Invaders from Mars* distinguishes itself for the pronounced adolescent point of view, centering the story on young David (played by Jimmy Hunt). Certainly, director Steven Spielberg had Menzies' movie in mind when he fashioned his box office blockbuster *E.T.* (1982). It is interesting to compare Don Siegel's *Invasion of the Body Snatchers* with the Menzies rendition in the calibration of human disguise and the sharp angularity of Menzies' production design. David's parents, first to be possessed by the aliens, are bluntly ill tempered and foul. There is no subtlety to their transformation whatsoever. By contrast, the friends and lover of the hero in Siegel's film are more skillfully impersonated, altogether shrewd, and it takes a passionless kiss for the hero to realize that he lost his love to the pod people.

The Menzies film begins with David, the precocious twelve year old son of an atomic scientist, waking in the middle of night to the sight and sound of a flying saucer descending into the ground. David pulls his father out of bed to investigate outside their home. To David's revulsion, his father returns from the fenced off bog in a hideous disposition and sporting a diminutive mark on the back of his neck. In short order, David's mother and a neighborhood girl both transform. Further, the girl seems to have started a fire to her basement and the camera catches her wearing a slight smile. David's paranoia, understandably, gets the better of him. No one in the community buys his phantasmagoric account of the visiting space ship and the scarring on victims' necks. David, having lost his composure, is escorted to the police station, designed in smart expressionistic lines and spare detail in the mode of a Joseph Cornell box. Indeed, the careful production design and theatrical lighting throughout lend pedigree to the film's abstracted dreamscape.[7] Although the police captain seems to be possessed by one of the alien invaders, David has a gentle interview with Dr. Pat Blake, a lovely doctor with city health services. She softens David's harsh ride and establishes immediate rapport with the boy. In essence, Dr. Blake becomes the surrogate mother for David as she takes him to a reassuring father figure, the astronomer Dr. Stuart Kelston.

Thanks to Kelston's professional efforts, there is support for David's allegations. Through the observatory's telescope, Keltson and David spy the security commander of the nearby atomic lab descending into a massive sink hole. By hunting underground, David discovers a forbidding Martian's head and tentacles encased in a glass bowl. The aliens are planning to undermine the town's atomic rocket experiments and eliminate everyone. The U.S. Army is now engaged in full combat with the Martian forces underground and we see David and the American soldiers take flight after planting explosives within the saucer. The explosion marks the triumph of American resistance. Diplomacy would never have succeeded in this dangerous international affair.

In common with *Invasion of the Body Snatchers*, *Invaders from Mars* has been edited with two endings. Both films make adjustments with the final perception of their respective protagonists. At issue is the validation of the nightmare for the solitary individual.[8] The facile epilogue in most versions of Menzies' film has the boy back in his bedroom as thunder hits the sky. David's parents comfort him, saying that he had a bad dream. With another roll of thunder, David—alone again—sees a flying saucer land softly near the sandy field just outside his home. The other version features the story ending with the explosion of the space vehicle.

Viewing the cinematic science fiction invasions of the 1950s, and taking into account the virulent McCarthyism that fed much of the decade, one can speculate about the degree to which the American public found either catharsis or further hysteria in attending such movies. Analyzing the narrative details of an identity (and corporal body) lost to an aggressive nemesis yields several stark conclusions. Taken as social metaphor, American life suddenly turns brittle and inauthentic. Nothing can be accepted on face value anymore and the public trust is irrevocably damaged. One's neighbor or loved one might be a spy. Taken more literally in the context of the space race, American society had embraced an insular position rather than an expansive civic contract in the spirit of Rousseau.

As an art designer, Menzies had been honored with an Academy Award for *Gone with the Wind* (1939), and he was also the uncredited art designer for the cult film *The Thief of Bagdad* (1940).[9] Like Ed Wood, Menzies had no hesitation to make use of stock army film clips to stretch his action scenes. But to his credit, Menzies concocted weirdly engaging special effects in the subterranean war scenes and UFOs in flight. There are several moments in the film that thoroughly jar an audience today. For example, David's father hits him quite hard on the head, and there is an extended scene with David behind bars in the police station. One should not completely dismiss the film's symbolism of child abuse or the tertiary sexual aura radiating from Dr. Pat Blake, who comforts David as both she and the boy are brought underground in the ensuing battles.

Like *Invasion of the Body Snatchers*, *Invaders from Mars* was remade decades later (with direction by Tobe Hooper) only to fail at the box office, perhaps proving that Communism in the 1980s was seriously on the wane. For those baby boomers who recall watching Menzies' film in the theatre or later on television, *Invaders from Mars* was a scarring experience and a private one for tender aged children. The intense, visceral experience may contribute to the theory of individualization and maturation.[10] The cruelty and isolation inherent in David's journey come as a result of disassociated parents. In addition, the requisite 'duck and cover' nuclear drills in the public school corridors during the late 1950s did little to allay the amorphous fears of American children.

The Incredible Shrinking Man (1957)

Director Jack Arnold had built a solid reputation with many drive-in theatre films: *It Came from Outer Space* (1953), *The Creature from the Black Lagoon* (1954), and *High School Confidential* (1958). These eccentrically delightful black and white features were very much of the same fabric as their respective titles, and the playful fun derived from these Arnold films was firmly rooted in the 1950s B movie mentality. Each of these films became popular campy classics within a span of fifteen years. He went on to maintain a high profile in television, from *The Bionic Woman* to *The Love Boat*. His voluminous credits project a solid, workmanlike proficiency from the 1950s to the 1980s. However, there is masterly quality to his esteemed, melancholic *The Incredible Shrinking Man* that goes far beyond its special effects high concept. *The Incredible Shrinking Man* was that extremely rare period product that did away with the requisite creature from outer space, the animal kingdom, or nearby graveyard. One can glean a genuine existential pain in the mythic rendering of the human race's insignificance. Based on the critically praised Richard Matheson novel *The Shrinking Man* (1956), Arnold and Matheson (as screenwriter) surpassed the imaginative laziness inherent in quickly-spun horror movies and invested an intellectual sensibility to Arnold's eye-catching storytelling. Matheson sold the book to Universal-International, stipulating that he would be assigned to execute the screenplay, although Richard Alan Simmons was also listed on the shooting script.[11] Upon its premiere, the film was complimented for highly creative camera work and potent special effects.

Typical of the era and science fiction film genre, the loudly explicit movie title sells to a 1950s audience. However, the assured, focused direction and screenplay succeed with a discreet understatement of a man in peril. Moreover, unlike many fantasy films from the period, the fierce terror of Communism plays no role in this tale. Matheson's screenplay has a finely descriptive, contemplative voice in balance with the outward shocks of a human body and soul in philosophic crisis. The film relies forcefully and sometimes intrusively on character Scott Carey's voiceover narration, which is a vestige of Matheson's novel speaking unapologetically. In contrast to the film, Matheson's novel seems a- stream-of-consciousness blending of time, mood, and memory in Scott's atomized identity. Matheson has worked extensively in this genre for film, television and in his novels.[12] The concept of Matheson's cosmic victimization owes much to Franz Kafka's masochistic imagination. On the other hand, Matheson's application of realism keeps the work from reading as postmodern and sexualized as Philip Roth's novel of transformation, *The Breast* (1972). Common to all three novelists and axiomatic, the physiological crisis is happening to one man only and not an entire community. In that regard, the existential injury that results is far more acute and deadly. Although Matheson's book cuts back and forth in time with respect to the protagonist's physical plight (anchored inside a doll's house), the film is cleanly divided into three distinct dramatic acts, with the first act the briefest on screen—and seemingly the most ordinary. The powerfully visual third act, being thoroughly surreal and nightmarish, can be seen as a film unto itself.

The Incredible Shrinking Man opens with Scott and his wife Louise vacationing aboard a boat. Spoiling their ideal holiday, a mysterious cloud of particles overtakes the vehicle. Louise is down in the cabin hull while Scott, in bathing suit, lounges on deck. There is a luminous residue on his body. He later notices that his shirts no longer fit him and he feels not quite himself. Apparently, Scott's exposure to the ocean cloud was more problematic than his wife's, for in a matter of weeks, Scott becomes smaller. Thus begins act two. After a string of medical exams, Scott learns that something has reduced his system's capacity to maintain nitrogen, calcium, and phosphorus. It is assumed that the cloud was some form of radioactive agent. No precedent exists in medical annals for this body condition. Losing an inch each week, he cannot hold his job and becomes estranged from Louise. In Scott's dramatic physical transformation, he also experiences a subtle shift in his chauvinism toward Louise. He now has become dependent on her in many ways. Further, in order for Scott to stay solvent, he has to capitalize on selling his life story to the media. Scott's discernible depression is in direct proportion to his pronounced emasculation as an American man at the height of his powers in career and in marriage. The parallel between Scott's sudden inadequacy and America's crushed reaction to the successful space launch in 1957 of Sputnik 1 resonates; the film's accidental timing lends significance to Arnold's achievement.

At first, it seems that the medical treatment abates the shrinkage when Scott stands no higher than a six-year old boy. The doctor alerts Scott that his body has created an "anti-cancer," a counter-response to the strain of insecticide and radioactive material he had absorbed in the boating incident. This chronological interruption creates false optimism for Scott and the audience. In addition, Scott experiences some temporary pleasure in this frightening ordeal when he meets an attractive dwarf named Clarice, a circus performer who helps Scott to normalize his self-perception. There is an instant connection, and Scott is thoroughly appreciative. Clarice presents an interesting romantic triangle for him, since she is now the perfect mate and Louise represents the past. The film does not investigate the complications of the triangle, however, because Scott's medical condition returns and ends his brief affair with Clarice. His male sensitivity has transformed as well and the earlier dominance of Scott's personality has devolved into disquieting fragility.

The filmic transition from act two to act three is blunt and effective. Standing alone from the preceding narrative, it becomes a film within a film. Scott resides inside a new home. The camera pulls back and we see that he occupies a dollhouse. In a tragic, inadvertent action, one evening Louise leaves the house but lets the outside cat in. Scott's life is threatened by the menacing pet but he manages to escape into the home's cellar. Upon returning, Louise presumes her husband was eaten by the cat. The ensuing final weeks in Scott's diminishing life involve finding food for sustenance and fighting off a spider. Scott's make-shift clothing is a cross between a raggedy dress and Roman toga. With sewing needle and thread as his spear and rope, he has to resort to the most primitive forms of combat and survival as though he were a caveman. While Scott is tri-umphant with the predator spider in the climax of act three, the immediate future holds nothing tangible for a man smaller than a thimble. Scott ends his time on screen articulating an epiphany about his new place within eternity.

Filmed in less than two months for a modest $800,000, *The Incredible Shrinking Man* avoids some of the interesting narrative complications found in Matheson's novel, such as a five-year old daughter and physical threats from teenage hoods.[13] Male inadequacy was not a major theme in the 1950s, but Ar-nold's film gave a lasting interpretation on an underplayed idea in America cinema.

Notes:

1   Michael Medved and Harry Medved, *The Golden Turkey Awards* (New York: Perigee/Putnam, 1980), 177-181.

2   Anthony Summers, *Official and Confidential: The Secret Life of J. Edgar Hoover* (New York: G.P. Putnam's Sons, 1993), 254-258.

3   Jeffrey Sconce, *'Trashing' the Academy: Taste, Excess, and Emerging Politics of Cinematic Style;* Leo Braudy and Marshall Cohen, eds., *Film Theory and Criticism* (New York: Oxford University Press, 2004), 550.

4   Richard Barrios, *Screened Out: Playing Gay in Hollywood from Edison to Stonewall* (New York: Routledge, 2003), 236.

5   Danny Peary, *Cult Movies 3* (New York: Fireside, 1988), 100.

6   Peary, *Cult Movies 3*, 100.

7   Vivian Sobchanck, *Screening Space: The American Science Fiction Film* (New Brunswick, New Jersey: Rutgers University Press, 1999), 87.

8   Bill Warren, *Keep Watching the Skies! American Science Fiction Movies of the Fifties Vol. 1* (Jefferson & London: McFarland. 1982), 120.

9   Warren, *Keep Watching the Skies! American Science Fiction Movies of the Fif-ties Vol. 1*, 117.

10   J.P. Telotte, *Science Fiction Film (Genres in American Cinema)* (Cambridge: Cambridge University Press, 2001), 48-49.

11   Bill Warren, *Keep Watching the Skies! American Science Fiction Movies of the Fifties Vol. 1* (Jefferson & London: McFarland. 1982), 353.

12   Karl French and Philip French, *Cult Movies* (New York: Billboard Books, 2000), 115.

13   Bill Warren, *Keep Watching the Skies! American Science Fiction Movies of the Fifties Vol. 1* (Jefferson & London: McFarland. 1982), 354.

Chapter Five
Films from the 1960s

America in the 1960s shifted radically as if time were tectonic plates under co-lossal realignment. Although it is an overstatement to identify the decade as a reign of youth (or misguided youth), nearly seventy million baby boomers en-tered their teen and young adult years. This demographic also presented a dis-cernible rebellion from the conformist limitations and conservative mindset of the previous decade. Helped by the election of the youngest president in history, the 1960s began with clear symbols of new thought and energetic possibilities aligned with a younger generation. As the decade began, Alan Shepard became the first American in space. Elvis Presley enjoyed his heralded return from the military service just as the national music scene was on the verge of great inno-vative sounds featuring Motown, the British rock invasion, and folk. Bob Dy-lan's poetic lyrics ignited an entire generation into the political arena, even though his audience base began quite small. Despite the explosive 1962 Cuban missile crisis, the decade assumed a modicum of optimism until the tragic assas-sination of President John Kennedy in 1963. Recovery for the nation's psyche was not quick enough, as tremendous social events embroiled every state in the union. The formidable civil rights movement started peacefully, led by Dr. Mar-tin Luther King and many other black church leaders, but the maelstrom thatfol-lowed undermined the best altruistic efforts. At the same time, women's rights forced new social awareness. School prayer was declared unconstitutional by the Supreme Court. The early involvement in the Vietnam conflict became unbeara-bly turbulent during the Lyndon Johnson's White House years. Youth's hold on popular music, from The Beatles to Jimi Hendrix, broadcast on FM radio, and the explosive hippie revolution generated widespread recreational drug use, sexual freedom helped by the birth control pill, and more irreverent and frank motion pictures from Hollywood, *Guess Who's Coming to Dinner?*(1967) to *Midnight Cowboy* (1969). The New York theatre scene evolved with the addi-tion of unorthodox and idiosyncratic off Broadway shows complementing the more expensive and mainstream Broadway fare. Influential novels and literature of the period include Ken Kesey's *One Flew Over the Cuckoo's Nest* (1962) and works by Susan Sontag, Kurt Vonnegut, Saul Bellow, Betty Friedan, Joseph Heller, Eldridge Cleaver, and John Updike. In the sports world, Cassius Clay became Muhammad Ali and illuminated the boxing kingdom and American culture in untold ways. Draft resisters grew exponentially and college campuses assumed a significant role as a hotbed of political protest against the Vietnam War.

Contributing to the dark clouds of 1960s social activism were the assassina-tions of Medgar Evers, Dr. King, Malcolm X, and Senator Robert Kennedy. The

youth protest movement and the mounting pains of the Vietnam War succeeded
in discouraging President Johnson from seeking the 1968 nomination for re-
election. The decade's technological capstone was realized by the televised 1969
lunar landing and breathtaking moon walk by Neil Armstrong and Buzz Aldrin.
The 1969 Stonewall riots in New York's Greenwich Village triggered the gay
rights movement. Stunning many political analysts, Hollywood actor Ronald
Reagan won the1966 gubernatorial election in California and Richard Nixon
finally found his way to the White House two years later. Symbolically, the
oppositional twin heads of rock culture erupted to fuel the popular imagination
about good and evil within America. In the summer of 1969, the world famous
Woodstock festival in upstate New York brought out a message of peace, coop-
eration, and love. Four months later, on the other side of the country, the Alta-
mont Free Concert, featuring the Rolling Stones and a Hells Angels security
team, degenerated into a debacle with the death of a young black man, Meredith
Hunter, by one of the biker sercurity guards.

Psycho (1960)

In Robert Bloch's morally unpleasant novel *Psycho,* published in 1959, the
creation of Norman Bates was based on the notorious serial killer Ed Gein, who
inspired Alfred Hitchcock's film, and decades later, inspired the fictional "Buf-
falo Bill" of Jonathan Demme's celebrated *The Silence of the Lambs* (1991).
Gein's heinous crimes were discovered two years prior to the novel *Psycho's*
first printing. Despite the fact that horror fiction at the time was normally ig-
nored by the literary cognoscenti, Bloch's book received flattering reviews and
postings in *The New York Times Book Review* and *The Times Herald.* Anthony
Boucher wrote in *The New York Times Book Review*: "[Bloch] is more chillingly
effective than any writer might reasonably be expected to be . . . [and] demonstrates that a believable history of mental illness can be more icily terrifying
than all the arcane horrors summoned up by a collaboration of Poe and Love-
craft."[1] Alfred Hitchcock purchased the rights to the novel anonymously (report-
edly for $9,000) and was incorrectly told at the time that Bloch was unavailable
to adapt the screenplay.[2] The director eventually hired Joseph Stefano to complete the script. To many readers and critics, Bloch's book was even more violent than the Hitchcock film. The specifics of the atrocities are given lavish,
graphic details. If this is any consolation, the young heroine gets beheaded in the
shower and does not suffer the hypnotic stabbing we witness in the film.

In Bloch's macabre rendering, mass murderer Bates is a self-absorbed,
heavy-set, middle-aged man, a reprobate who drinks and listens to Beethoven.[3]
There was little in this depiction with which the genral reader could sympathize.
As stated in several interviews, Stefano decided to soften the killer by making
him a young, sadly vulnerable, handsome man. Once we get past the carefully
specific introduction of Norman Bates in Bloch's book, we follow the same
crime narrative as depicted in the film: Mary Crane arrives at Bates Motel. She

is murdered by Bates' mother in the shower, and Bates must dispose of the body.

As in the fictional Bates' chronicles, Gein's initial victim was named Mary. Like Norman, Gein also dressed up in ladies garments but he allegedly sported the breasts and skins of his mother. Similarly, Bates' chronicles, Gein lived in a very remote, sparsely populated community, Plainfield, Wisconsin—the very state that subsequently produced another cannibalistic serial killer, Jeffrey Dahmer. And like the fictional Bates character, once Gein was incarcerated he was virtually an amnesiac.[4] The memory of these killings becomes the unwanted morbid legacy of the witness; both the reader and the film viewer of *Psycho* take on one added ordeal which serves perhaps as the indelible irony to a psychotic killer's horrifying, crime spree.

In Hitchcock's rendition, office secretary Marion Crane hopes her adulterous boyfriend, hardware store manager Sam, will marry her now that she has embezzled $40,000 from her real estate firm. On impulse, Marion packs up, and drives from Phoenix to visit Sam, who lives in California. Marion, played astutely by Janet Leigh, does not exude criminal attitude or wanton airs. On the contrary, she appears upstanding and respectable—one's next door neighbor. A storm forces her to leave the interstate highway just a few miles from Sam's home. She checks into Bates motel—a dreary and vacant row of banal cabins. Marion learns from Norman Bates that that his business has been hurting with the intrusion of the new interstate. Although a shy young introvert, Norman shows keen interest in Marion and offers her a meal before retiring for the night. A disconcerting note, she manages to eavesdrop on Norman in an argument with his unseen mother.

During the meal in Norman's office, he conveys to Marion the travails of caring for an invalid parent who is uncompromisingly domineering. Marion feels charitable toward him and commiserates. She oversteps an unseen boundary by gently suggesting that Norman's mother could be given institutional care. Saying this, Marion has sealed her fate. Back in her motel room, Marion rethinks her decision to run off with the stolen money. She will go back to Phoenix the next day and reclaim her former life. Marion disrobes for her shower as Norman makes his way back to the main house where his mother dwells. Moments later, Marion is savagely attacked in the motel shower by a long figure in a drab dress wielding a knife. The killer exits and soon Norman, shocked, enters the scene of the murder. He is compelled to protect his mother from the crime she apparently had committed. Norman disposes of Marion's body. Besides scaring audiences out of their wits, Hitchcock has broken a major rule in feature films by discarding his Hollywood star Janet Leigh so early in the film.

Marion's sister Lila seeks Sam in Fairville, California as she searches for Marion. Sam is unsettled to know that Marion has been missing and is suspected of embezzlement. Additionally, Marion's employer hires an investigator, Arbogast, to track Marion down. He follows her trail to Bates Motel. Arbogast tricks Norman into admitting that Marion visited his facility and that he lives with his invalid mother. Denied permission to speak with Mrs. Bates, Arbogast intends to slip into the Bates residence—an action that leads to the second on-screen murder. In the meantime, Lila assumes Marion's role as the female protagonist in *Psycho*.

The sheriff informs Lila and Sam that Norman's mother died a decade ago after poisoning her lover and herself. Sparked by this information, Lila and Sam register for a night at Bates Motel. Lila sneaks up to the private house as Sam attempts to distract Norman at the motel desk. Norman senses the scheme and assaults Sam. The dramatic climax has Lila descending into in the dingy cellar to find Mrs. Bates seated with her back to the camera. Lila discovers that Norman's mother is a hideous cadaver. Rushing to the scene in the haggard old lady's dress is Norman, holding the gleaming knife aloft. But on this occasion, the killer is subdued by Sam arriving in the nick of time. A psychiatrist explains in the film's coda that pre-teen Norman had murdered his mother and her boyfriend; having exhumed her body years later, Bates took possession of his mother's identity. The film closes with Bates now devoid of any Norman personality.

Many film taboos were broached in *Psycho*, including the first depiction of an open toilet in a scene, deviant transvestite behavior, the depiction of a respectable woman wearing a sexy brassiere, and the killing of a naked heroine who merits a full narrative arc.[5] Hitchcock exploited the erosion of Hollywood's Production Code by filming what had heretofore been cinematically unthinkable. Hitchcock's minimal budget dictated his employment of his television crew and the use of simple broadcast studio practices such as tight indoor shots, cheap sets, and small cast to powerful effect. With *Psycho*, Hitchcock moved from elevated suspense thrillers and fathered the modern horror film. The visceral impact of Bates' taxidermy and gothic design elements within a black and white film unnerves the viewer continually. Anthony Perkins delivered the most definitive psychotic performance of the decade. Bernard Hermann's subliminal score for violins captured to perfection the staccato violence and tightly strung pathology of Norman Bates. Janet Leigh portrayed the compelling dual image of feminine hedonism and human contrition until the moment of her death.

Hitchcock's much analyzed, infamous shower sequence terrorized the world and, according to Leigh's biography, made showering, subsequent to filming of *Psycho*, extremely uncomfortable for her. Surely, Leigh was not alone with this phobia. In the quake of the film's release, businesswomen would not travel to hotels alone and women would shower at friends' homes. Even more provocative to society, the phenomenon of the deranged serial killer became part of the national landscape just after the completion of the interstate highway system. Hitchcock was indicting America in part for a transient, motel culture.[6] In an odd way, the film intimated the emergence of Lee Harvey Oswald and other lone assassins of the 1960s. The majority of film critics reviled British director Hitchcock for what they considered a foul, neo-pornographic venture. Still, the film was a popular sensation and signaled a new direction in the genre of realistic horror. The studio marketing campaign demanded that the reviewers not reveal the movie's conclusion and many theatres would not allow late seating after the film began. Coincidentally, Michael Powell's *Peeping Tom*, a sharply controversial British cult serial killer film released months before *Psycho*, iterated the themes of voyeurism, sexual murder, and child abuse found in Hitchcock's spectacular shocker.

Faster, Pussycat! Kill! Kill! (1966)

Bonanza was a staple of television from 1959 until 1973. Along with *Gunsmoke*, *Bonanza* dominated all Westerns on the family tube. The show is set in the American west and tracks the masculine adventures and self-reliance of the Cartwright family. Owner of the immense ranch called Ponderosa, three-time widower Ben Cartwright maintains his property with his three grown sons Adam, Hoss, and Little Joe. The Cartwright men pride themselves on their environmentalism and their moral center. Women never intruded into their lives beyond one or two episodes.[7]

Filmed for an estimated $45,000, Russ Meyer's demented sexploitation film *Faster, Pussycat! Kill! Kill!* (his eleventh film) extrapolates the Cartwright men one hundred years later.[8] It is a cruel evolution, to be sure. The modern day clan is thoroughly miserable and lonely. Meyer's analogue for Ben Cartwright is a nameless miser trapped in a wheelchair. Instead of having three sons, the old man has but two (*Bonanza* lost Adam in the final broadcast years). Kirk has brains and the handsome Vegetable has brawn. They stand in for Adam and Hoss Cartwright respectively. Meyer accepted the fact that the youngest son—Little Joe—was shipped to another hit television show, *Little House on the Prairie*. As far as ecology and moral order, there are no vestiges of either on this remote Nevada ranch.

A Russ Meyer film features unforgettable, buxom women as far removed from reality as can be. On the screen these women are frightening yet comedic. They are Nietzschian women, in large part, due to their outlaw will and their freedom from empathy, and they are the creatures Nietzsche had warned: "Going to thy woman? Do not forget thy whip!" The aggressive feminine force that ignites Meyer's story and wreaks havoc on the modern day "Ponderosa" ranch is vicious, athletic Varla, played by Tura Satana. She is more than a great killer shark who cannot stop her predator ways. She gloats about every conquest, making every event a barroom contest. Her partners in crime are Rosie and Billie, who are caught in an ongoing girls' feud. All professional go-go dancers, these three women love to race their roadsters in the wide expanses of the desert. The film's first stab at comedy occurs when an unsuspecting Tommy and Linda—a "square" couple—cross their path. Wearing plaid Bermuda shorts, Tommy—in his hot sports car—runs time trials, much to Varla's amusement. She ridicules his manhood and manipulates him to race against her. Varla cheats and wipes out Tommy. They fight *mano a mano*; Tommy's unguarded efforts are no match for Varla's karate and killer instinct. After Tommy's murder, the ladies kidnap a very stunned Linda.

It may be Meyer's personal joke to transpose Varla, Rosie, and Billie to the fabled "Ponderosa," but one senses some inspired madness in the plotline. Neither the sexist gang of women nor the hapless family of Meyer men has any virtue. Varla learns from a gas station attendant (Meyer frequently features gas station attendants in his films) that a horrid old local man had received a lottery size settlement following a rail accident. That carrot is enough to warrant a side trip to the nearby ranch and contrive a plan to steal the patriarch's cash.

Linda, along for the sadistic ride, complicates the visit to the ranch. The gang concocts a story explaining why Linda is hog tied: "Linda's boyfriend died in an accident and she is now deranged." Varla, Rosie, and Billie "were hired by Linda's rich parents to return her without press and police interference." Varla's lie is a ludicrous proposition, but that doesn't dissuade the "Ponderosa" men. The women are invited to lunch.

Because in the hyperbolic world of Russ Meyer sexual impulses are stronger than story needs, Billie makes a play for the hulking Vegetable. The old man, now alone with hostage Linda, seizes his opportunity to grope her. She runs away but is intercepted by Kirk, the rational member of the ranch. He drives her back against her protests. Another director might fashion this tale from Linda's point of view in an account of her survival against all odds. However, Meyer's focus is on America's vacant and godless "no man's land." To Meyer, Linda will earn her life back, paid for with deeply etched scars.

Eventually, Varla orders Rosie and Billie to kill Linda and the three ranchers in order to find the fortune. Billie refuses and Varla stabs her to death. This infuriates Vegetable. The two women knock down the old geezer which releases the stash of cash hidden in the wheel chair. Vegetable knifes Rosie, killing her cold. Varla slams the truck into Vegetable. Vegetable's upper body strength braced against a wall, withstands Varla's vehicular attack. When Varla discovers Kirk and Linda far from the ranch, Varla nearly murders Kirk with her bare hands. Timid Linda saves Kirk by jumping into the truck and driving headlong into Varla. The audience is surprised to witness Varla lose her invincibility as much as seeing Linda find her own fighting instinct. Plainly, luck and not moral necessity helped Linda and Kirk outlast the bitchiest of all 1960s monsters. Yet the psychological ghosts from this day will undoubtedly haunt them for years to come.

Why would Russ Meyer vandalize the legacy of the shining Cartwright television family? Was *Bonanza* too inviting and broad a target for the reigning king of early soft porn? Beyond the ironic camp humor of his entire film output, Meyer is signaling his vision of undisguised sexual warfare and, to a lesser extent, class consciousness as a political metaphor for this nation's greed, pathology, and self-regard. Further, Meyer is suggesting that the symbolic head of the American family has an estate that is unearned and that this figure is usually lecherous. Most revealing, Meyer equates the passive immorality of the father with the aggressive venality of the murderess Varla.

Linking the antecedent drama, *Bonanza*, to another famous television show that became an unlikely descendent and "corrective" to *Faster, Pussycat—Charlie's Angels* (1976-81) was a savvy response to Meyer's Bad Girls. The do-good, ultra-capable, crime-fighting women in *Charlie's Angels* deliver the fully inverted image of the malicious Meyer women and respond faithfully to the directions of the disembodied, patriarch voice of Charlie. In an implicit, cute manner, Charlie rules the roost, whereas Meyer's Bad Girls need not heed anyone's bidding. God help the man who tries to bark one order at Varla. And yet, all things considered, the Meyer's "angels" appear closer to reality than their television counterparts. When Drew Barrymore devised the idea to imagine *Charlie's Angels* on the big screen two decades after the television show was cancelled, her commercial strategy was quite perceptive. This candy stripe rendition of Girl Power had renewed appeal for today's audience. Barrymore and her producing team enhanced the kick-ass sass of the female martial arts trio, all the while continuing to camp up the ditzy excesses of what really is at root— ersatz sorority suitemates fighting over the bathroom. The *Angels* were having their cake and eating it too.

Russ Meyer, despite his self-imposed soft porn label, holds a singular position in the film industry, bridged the conformist 1950s and the bold, pace-setting 1970s. His eccentricity served as his major strength and his major limitation. Film critic Danny Peary concurs with director John Waters (*Pink Flamingos,* 1972) that Meyer is the "Eisenstein of sex films" who has helped married couples add a little zing to a dull bedroom.[9] He began a professional career as a Playboy magazine photographer and glided into semi-naked 16-millimeter narrative effortlessly. Undoubtedly, Meyer had an overwhelming influence on the crown prince of bad taste, John Waters. Waters has been generous with praise for *Faster Pussycat* and other Meyer classics. Likewise, one wonders if the Philip Roth novel, *The Breast* (1972), is a quiet homage to Franz Kafka or Russ Meyer.

In the 1970s and 1980s, it had been a well established practice how to guarantee a sellout weekend film series on college campuses by featuring either *Faster Pussycat* or the other 1970 Meyer hit—*Beyond the Valley of the Dolls* (often called BVD). Of course, *Beyond the Valley of the Dolls'* sick, dunderhead script came from *Chicago Sun* film critic and long time Meyer admirer, Roger Ebert. Many cult cineastes complain that it is impossible to rent any Russ Meyer film from Blockbuster or Netflix. A Meyer title conveys something illicit and forbidden; only very recently has Amazon.com listed the Meyer repertoire. Purchase prices for Meyer films are much higher than the average DVD from MGM or Paramount Pictures.

Russ Meyer maintained full ownership and near-exclusive distribution up until his death in 2004. It is interesting to note that *The New York Times* gave Meyer a very respectful obituary. He had flirted with Hollywood twice and retreated to the low radar realm of independent filmmaking long before Sundance, the Independent Film Channel, and Independent Film Awards became fashionable. In 1977, the manager of the punk rockers, Sex Pistols, contracted Meyer to shoot the group in a film called *Who Killed Bambi?*, but the project fizzled.[10] Meyer stayed away from explicit pornography because of his quixotic quest for some respectable artistic stature. Indeed, Meyer was a genuine American auteur. Many suburban teenagers from the 1960s may recall hanging outside for hours along the chain link fence of their local drive-in theatre just to view a bevy of nude Meyer actresses. Meyer instinctively knew that American men will happily remain teenagers after they outgrow their love of westerns. Goodbye *Bonanza*, kiss that horse farewell.

Perhaps most telling is Hollywood screenwriter William Goldman tribute to Russ Meyer in Goldman's best selling *Adventures in the Screen Trade*: "Is there then no American auteur director? Perhaps there is one. One man who thinks up his own stories and produces his pictures and directs them too. And also serves as his own cinematographer. Not to mention he also does his own editing. All this connected with an intensely personal and unique vision of the world. That man is Russ Meyer."[11]

Rosemary's Baby (1968)

The film version of Ira Levin's best selling suspense novel, *Rosemary's Baby*, spawned a succession of prestigious Hollywood horror films like *The Exorcist* (1973) and *The Omen* (1976) that carried a clear message to audiences about the cunning challenge of evil. From a philosophical standpoint, such a statement was extremely disconcerting and revelatory about the period. Inherent in the new Hollywood declaration was the profound suggestion that good, in some fashion, was enabling evil. Was the American public rethinking the failing U.S. war in Asia and the sustained difficulties in race relations stateside? Was the film an unconscious commentary on the recent assassinations of Robert Kennedy, Martin Luther King, and Malcolm X? And was *Rosemary's Baby*'s commercial success an impending provocation to Charles Manson's homicidal actions against Polanski's pregnant wife, Sharon Tate, within the year following the film's release? In light of cult films adherence to transgression and moral shock, it is unthinkable to exclude the Manson connection in the study of this landmark movie.

Alfred Hitchcock declined the movie rights to Levin's novel, allowing producer/director William Castle the opportunity to obtain them for $150,000. The discernible best-selling pedigree of the Levin book clashed with Castle's drive-in horror films; Castle enlisted Paramount vice president Robert Evans to choose the director. Evans had admired Polanski's *Repulsion* (1965) and felt that the Polish director would be brilliant.[10]

Rosemary Woodhouse's filmic story functions adroitly in two opposing directions at least halfway to the terrifying finale, the birth of her baby son. Either she is losing her rational faculties or she has fallen into the clutches of a powerful satanic cult. Then again, it is possible that Rosemary has succumbed to some functional irrationality while under a group's demonic spell or under the pressures of marriage and a difficult pregnancy. While the book suspends the key surprises until the end, the film version unmasks the coven next door much earlier in the narrative. The film asks its audience to follow the fatalism of the plot rather than play amateur detective along with Rosemary. Roman Polanski's first Hollywood film is that rare, well dressed, horror tale that maintains high etiquette and avoids gore. We are given many suggestive abnormal images and morbid dramatic moments. The script is quite understated, restrained, and witty; the direction holds a gripping intelligence to the *mise-en-scène*. In addition, no other film from this period encapsulates in metaphor the diabolical implosion of American idealism and innocence. Rosemary, in her decency and simple trust, represents a large section of the country. The film, like the Ira Levin novel, concludes with Rosemary crashing a respectable baby shower. In her hand is a large kitchen knife. Unlike the vast majority of showers, this one failed to invite the mother yet welcomes the birth of the anti-Christ.

The film depicts a young couple moving into an apartment in Manhattan's elegant and gothic Bramford House (the exteriors were the actual Dakota) on the Upper West Side. Rosemary, as portrayed by Mia Farrow, appears innocent and unusually naïve. Rosemary's husband, Guy, is an ambitious actor lacking substantial theatrical credits. John Cassevetes renders Guy with far less purity than Rosemary possesses. The couple learns from their friend Edward Hutchins that the Bramford had a wild, sordid history of grisly incidents involving witchcraft. Their elderly, eccentric, new neighbors—Roman and Minnie Castevet (played exquisitely by Sidney Blackmer and Ruth Gordon)—take an active interest in the Woodhouse couple. In particular, Minnie Castevet latches onto Rosemary like a long-lost relation. To Minnie, Rosemary expresses her immediate desire to start a family. High appreciation is in order to envision actor Ruth Gordon balancing the malevolent Minnie with—a few short years later—the benign role of Maude (*Harold and Maude,* 1971).

Rosemary befriends a young woman, Terry, who lives with the Castevets. The two young women agree to do laundry together in the forbidding Bramford basement. Soon after, Rosemary and her husband find the police in front of the apartment; Terry had thrown herself out of the window. The Castevets seem utterly baffled by Terry's actions. The film later depicts Rosemary's strange dream of being raped by something inhuman.

After Guy spends more time with the elderly Roman—whose stories of world travel with a theatrical producer father intrigue Guy—his struggling acting career begins to swing toward success, just as he receives the news of his wife's pregnancy.

Rosemary's health deteriorates and her suspicions begin to rise. Minnie has been supplying her with a special prenatal herbal drink. Further, the Castevets have dispatched the famous Dr. Sapirstein to be Rosemary's obstetrician, and his manner is very paternalistic and odd. Guy is completely at ease with the Castavets and their group of elderly friends, and spends increasing amounts of time with them. Rosemary suffers in isolation. To make matters worse, she learns that her old friend Hutch has died rather mysteriously, but he had left her a package containing several incriminating books on witchcraft, one of which details covens in the Bramford. Her intelligent fragility ensures the very delicacy of the film's frightening premise.

Manhattan becomes an essential element of Polanski's composition. We are not in the witch haven of old Salem, but rather in a bright, modern metropolis. The disguise perpetrated by the members of the coven goes undetected by the civil authorities. We assume Rosemary is new to New York. Neither Rosemary nor Guy has any family or close friends in the region. The big city anonymity afforded to the Woodhouse couple presents an optimal arrangement for the Castevets in spinning their conspiratorial web. Not one prying neighbor can spot the spiritual disorder set loose on Rosemary. Even when Rosemary attempts, at the close of the film a brave act to return to her original physician, Dr. Hill, she is thwarted by Dr. Hill's respect for the eminent Dr. Sapirstein.

The film examines the shattering taboo of the sacred marriage oath. Guy betrays Rosemary. He has rationalized the betrayal in the most facile terms. Guy tells his wife in the film's final scene that the group has not hurt her and the Woodhouses can live a life of affluence and luxury. He implies that a common miscarriage would have rendered essentially the same results as the situation at hand. They can work toward having another child wholly their own, he reassures her. Despite the insensitivity of these remarks, Guy is expressing a future reality of maternity surrogacy decades before fertility clinics, in vitro procedures, and egg donors.

The moral uproar surrounding the film supported its box office success. The National Catholic Office for Motion Pictures faulted *Rosemary's Baby* for perverted depiction of icons and beliefs sacred to Christianity. Britain's Board of Film Censors ordered a deletion of the satanic rape scene because of "elements of kinky sex associated with black magic."[11]

Roman Polanski came to international attention with his first feature film, *A Knife in the Water* (1962), which received an Oscar nomination for Best Foreign Language Film. He made his way to Hollywood a few years following that initial success and the highly regarded British horror film *Repulsion*, starring Catherine Deneuve. His camp classic, *The Fearless Vampire Killers* (1967), which featured his wife, Sharon Tate, and himself, is his least characteristic work, due to the film's easy comedy style and general goofiness. After the murder of his wife by Manson and his coterie, Polanski returned to Europe but remained active as a filmmaker on both sides of the Atlantic. His version of *Macbeth* (1971) demonstrated haunting aspects of the extreme violence perpetrated by the Manson clan in Polanski's Beverly Hills home. His next major studio achievement was the *film noir* classic *Chinatown* (1974), starring Jack Nicholson. He also starred in and directed a chilling Kafkaesque tale entitled *The Tenant* (1976), about a Polish immigrant living in Paris.

Adding to Polanski's personal troubles eight years after the Tate killing, he was charged in Los Angeles of drugging and raping a thirteen year old girl during an alleged photo session. Subsequently, Polanski jumped bail and never returned to the U.S.[12] However, Polanski received another Oscar nomination for *Tess* (1979). His career seemed to languish until the making of the Holocaust drama *The Pianist* (2002), which garnered *Palme d'Or* at Cannes and an Academy Award for directing that same year. Throughout his long career, *Rosemary's Baby* emerges as his most penetrating analysis of conspiratorial horror and ontological pain.

A final thought about *Rosemary's Baby* and the unusual aura around the film's production and improbable afterlife: One of the urban legends about the film ties San Francisco Satanist Anton LaVey to the unofficial role of occult consultant to the creative team behind *Rosemary's Baby*. And despite official cast listings for the film, there are rumors that Anton LaVey had played the Devil in Polanski's movie. Again, according to the legend, LaVey's involvement led to the causality of bad luck to some of the cast and crew members. Far worse, LaVey was considered by a good many individuals to be the psychic, karmic link to the Manson atrocities.

Notes:

1   Stephen Rebello, *Alfred Hitchcock and the Making of Psycho* (New York: St. Martin's Press, 1990), 11.
2   Rebello, *Alfred Hitchcock and the Making of Psycho*, 11.
3   Robert Bloch, *Psycho* (New York: Tom Doherty Associates 1959), 186.
4   Stephen Rebello, *Alfred Hitchcock and the Making of Psycho* (New York: St. Martin's Press, 1990), 11.
5   Rebello, *Alfred Hitchcock and the Making of Psycho*, 47, 73.
6   Jonathan Freedman, Chapter Four in *Hitchcock's America,* eds. Jonathan Freedman and Richard Millington, (New York and Oxford: Oxford University Press, 1999), 78.
7   Jack Gould, "TV: Why 'Bonanza'?" *New York Times*, July 21, 1965.
8   David K Frasier, *Russ Meyer—The Life and Films* (Jefferson, North Carolina and London: McFarland & Company, 1997), 9-11.
9   Danny Peary, *Cult Movies 3* (New York: Fireside, 1988), 83.
10   J. Hoberman and Jonathan Rosenbaum, *Midnight Movies* (New York: Da Capo Press, 1983), 279.
11   William Goldman, *Adventures in the Screen Trade* (New York: Warner Books, 1984), 105.
12   Barbara Leaming, *Polanski, A Biography* (New York: Simon and Schuster, 1981), 82.
13   Leaming, *Polanski, A Biography*, 88.
14   Leaming, *Polanski, A Biography*, 188-191.

Chapter Six
Films from the 1970s

Reducing the 1970s into a period of America's overt narcissism and self-absorption would be a cruel caricature unfair to the decade, for certainly the gains of feminism and gay rights were redoubled from the 1960s and environmental issues found greater traction in the media and on the grass root level. Nonetheless, social critics such as Tom Wolfe had no hesitation calling this period the "Me decade" in full knowledge of disco parties, high priced cocaine chic, and conspicuous consumption. Many self-actualizing and meditation programs took root in every corner of the country. The remaining days of the Vietnam War were traced by governmental euphemisms betraying the evident truth of a failed foreign policy squandering thousands upon thousands of young soldiers' lives. On the other hand, the Nixon administration normalized relations with the Soviet Union and China in 1972. The constructive notion of détente began between Nixon and Russian leader Brezhnev in their ongoing disarmament talks. Soon after the 1972 re-election of Nixon, the Watergate drama exploded, which led to the toppling of Richard Nixon and many of his senior advisors. Gerald Ford's pardon of Nixon destroyed Ford's chance for winning the Presidency in 1976 and the impact of Watergate created an opportunity for the Democratic Party to regain the White House with a Washington outsider—Governor Jimmy Carter from Georgia. Recession and "stagflation" marred the Carter years despite his initial appeal as a plain spoken-commoner and peanut farmer. International oil price fluctuations led to a massive energy crisis and more substantial injury to Carter's leadership. The Iranian hostage crisis served as the final coffin nail to Carter's short political life on the national horizon and sparked Ted Koppel's influential *Nightline*, transforming television journalism. Dozens upon dozens of inner city communities were losing the war on crime and drugs. In the second half of the decade, New York City's financial situation suffered greatly and the city could not receive a federal bailout. On the popular music scene, classic rock, punk, and reggae shared stage with ubiquitious albums of discotheque cresting with the film and sound track for *Saturday Night Fever* (1977). Country music was making inroads into the northern metropolitan markets. Tennis pros Billie Jean King and Bobby Riggs captured headlines and cocktail chatter in a celebrated battle of the sexes match—the lady beat the gentleman. Perhaps the ugliest fashion lines and hair styles in the last fifty years came from this decade. NBC built a brilliant new youth audience with topically satirical *Saturday Night Live*. Pace-setting music videos began to circulate in anticipation of the next decade's MTV. Film directors Francis Ford Coppola, George Lucas, and Steven Spielberg dominated the decade with their respective blockbusters, *The Godfather* (1972), *Jaws* (1975), and *Star Wars* (1977). The phenomenon of midnight film showings in the nation's most sophisticated cities increased in a starling proportion to the decrease in suburban and rural drive-in movie theatres. Blaxploitation films such as *Foxy Brown* (1974), starring Pam Grier, and Bruce Lee martial arts films enriched a few new niches, centering on America's inner cities. Sexually notorious 1972 films *Deep Throat* and *Behind the Green Door* influenced high society's interest in "porn chic" and wore down American cinema's barriers to graphic content. John Updike, Joyce Carol Oates, Norman Mailer, Thomas Pynchon, E. L. Doctorow, Alice Walker, William Styron, Sam Shepard, Adrienne Kennedy, Maria Irene Fornes, and Erica Jong made strong impressions on the literary fiction scene, and *Washington Post* investigative journalists Robert Woodward and Carl Bernstein created unforgettable book sensations with *All the President's Men* (1974) and *The Final Days* (1977), depicting Nixon's fall from grace. The first rash of world terrorism struck America's consciousness with the shocking mass execution of Israeli Olympic athletes in Munich by a Palestinian group. The usurpation of Japanese automobile superiority over American manufacturers became apparent as the decade came to a close, and the United States would never regain domination in world auto markets. The Great Communicator, Ronald Reagan seemed thoroughly poised to take his place on the world stage after hammering President Carter in the 1980 electoral landside.

El Topo (1971)

If one can imagine Italian director Sergio Leone hallucinating heavily on psilocybin for a holiday weekend at the Esalen Institute in Big Sur, California to achieve self-realization and enlightenment, the madcap, eerie result might have been the narcissistic dreamscape known as *El Topo*. Known to many as the father of the stylish spaghetti western, Leone made unabashed, amoral epics out of hackneyed cowboy matinee film plots. The operatic Leone is best known for *The Good, the Bad and the Ugly* (1966) starring Clint Eastwood. It is hard not to think briefly of Sergio Leone when approaching any discussion of *El Topo*, with its large expanse of desert plains, lawless appetite among lone men, and the quasi-pornographic application of visual violence. Of the same generation as Leone, Alejandro Jodorowsky, visionary theatre director from Chile, began artistic life in puppet theatre, mime, and stage acting. These early phases of Jodorowsky's biography figure considerably in an appreciation of *El Topo*'s eclecticism and stagecraft. Moving to Paris, he founded the little recognized Panic Theatre movement with surrealist writers Roland Topor and Fernando Arrabal in 1962. He had worked with an impressive array of French theatre artists from Marcel Marceau to Maurice Chavalier.[1] All of Jodorowsky's movies were made in Mexico (Leone chose Spain and Italy), with Jodorowsky enjoying his own work as the featured actor and auteur. In recent years, after Jodorowsky left filmmaking, he turned his unbridled, imaginative energies to sundry spiritual practices and the interpretation of Tarot cards.

For the cognoscenti thirty seven years ago, *El Topo* became the first celebrated "midnight film" when it played six nights a week at Manhattan's Elgin
Theatre.[2] Word of mouth traveled quickly about *El Topo*'s intense *"trippiness"*
and the generous spiritual epiphany communicated to the chosen. The theatre,
like many urban cinema palaces of its time, allowed smoking in the upstairs
balcony and the twining of tobacco and marijuana smoke choked the air. Cult
film director Sam Fuller was a big admirer of *El Topo* and Jodorowsky's rich
tapestry of references to art, culture, and religion. Like Fuller, The Beatles' John
Lennon was extremely passionate about *El Topo* and The Beatles' manager,
Allen Klein, assisted the distribution of the film for late night bookings across
the United States.[3] Without the boost from Lennon and Klein, Jodorowsky
would probably never have found any sizable public audience. *El Topo* went on
to become the most controversial movie of the year and Jodorowsky's American
"midnight hour" debut invited both a large dose of repeat viewing by young
enthusiasts and acidic scorn by detractors of all ages who dropped into the Elgin.
El Topo luxuriates in a steady pulse of visual shocks ranging from physical
deformity to bestiality and employs a cinematic showmanship equivalent to
Leone's Italian colleague Federico Fellini's *Satyricon* (1969).

As the story begins, the figure of El Topo, played by Jodorowsky, rides the
open desert with his young, naked son. Immediately the filmmaker has signaled
his audience that we are not in the land of narrative realism. The opening image
of a fully clad horseman in black, cantering, holding an umbrella is arresting,
unsettling, and nearly comic. The boy hangs on for dear life. Could this be Abraham's proxy preparing to sacrifice Isaac? El Topo dismounts and instructs his
son to bury his first toy and his mother's photo—a rite of manhood and the first
perverse commandment. When father and son enter a remote town, we see evidence of genocide. Far worse than the sight of the slaughter is the unrelenting
sound of flies and miserable insects feasting on the dead. El Topo goes after the
killers and their military leader—the Colonel. The mistress of the Colonel persuades El Topo to run off with her at the expense of El Topo's naked son. Apparently this is a spontaneous decision forcing the boy to be abandoned to the
local monks. The boy will re-appear as a man in the second half of the story.

After copulating in the beautiful wilderness, El Topo is directed by the Colonel's mistress to eliminate the four grand Masters of this barren Mandala who
possess the universe. One infers that by killing these titans, El Topo assumes
their aggregate magical powers. To complicate matters, a Woman in Black attempts to win the mistress from El Topo. The plot's initial premise does not
drive the action forward as much as allow the disjointed spectacle of a cosmic
gunslinger dueling 'near immortals' and displaying alpha male sexuality. Certainly, Jodorowsky is taking what he needs from Christian passion and miracle
plays when convenient and reaches in the opposite direction to the Chinese
philosophy of Lao-tsu and Taoism. Adding the spaghetti Western killer enriches
the synthesis to a perfect comic book confection.

El Topo cannot match the first Master's quickness with a gun, but through
deception El Topo wins the encounter. In parallel violence, the mistress murders
two partnered men (one legless, the other armless) who were assistants to the

Master. One can sense some of the morbid affectation found in Jodorowsky's canvas in the depiction of two limbless individuals bound together like a walking totem pole. Afterwards, the mistress is drawn powerfully to her image in a reflecting pool. Repeating an act of vanity while embracing El Topo, the mistress is shot dead and El Topo collects the pieces of the mistress's broken mirror.

When El Topo approaches the second Master, we see a peculiar relationship of an unassuming magician living intimately with his mother. El Topo defeats this Master by subterfuge exploiting his opponent's mother. El Topo steals a metal ashtray from his victim and inserts the souvenir into his shirt. The next colorful Master wounds El Topo with a fatal shot, but miraculously the bullet collides with the metal ashtray. El Topo, on a good luck roll, kills his third Master. The remaining Master carries a butterfly net and undermines the threat of any material weapon aimed at him. El Topo cannot annihilate the Master. The fourth Master mocks death in front of El Topo by plunging a knife into himself—ostensibly completing the final task facing El Topo in his quest to conquer the mystic quartet. Death has no meaning now.

El Topo deliberates over his jounrey toward ultimate power, revisiting his aggressive steps from the onset of the film. He releases doves into the open sky. El Topo realizes the folly of his goal. We see him alone on a bridge. He is destitute. We sense that his soul is trapped uncomfortably between two worlds. The Woman in Black reappears and shoots his hands and feet. To conclude, she fires a last shot into El Topo's abdomen. It is as though Jodorwsky disguised Christ for a memorable cameo.[4] Rather than attend to him like Maria Magdalena, the mistress leaves El Topo for The Woman in Black. This launches the second half of the film from a chic platform of mystic lesbianism.

In part two, Jodorowsky's protagonist is now twenty years older, in monk's robe and shaved head, and humbled by his long penance. This identity is the antithesis of his former self. A loving, female dwarf tends to him; their home is a primitive cave among a community of disfigured dwarfs. Close by is an evil town that maintains and kills slaves for pleasure. El Topo and his mate perform vaudeville mime in the town's street for loose change. In a manner of speaking, Jodorowsky has reinvigorated Browning's *Freaks* to secure his film's back-ended plotting. Jodorowsky, like Browning before him, establishes two camps of society based on outward normality and deformity. Further, like Browning, Jodorowsky highlights his story with a mismatched romance between a full size, attractive individual and a dwarf. Symbolically, both directors touch on the notion and taboo of cultural miscegenation.

El Topo plans to construct a tunnel to free the downtrodden dwarfs who are forbidden to enter the town. An element of decency exists within the society of dwarfs while nothing decent can be found in the wealthy town. The townsfolk appear oppressed by a vapid, conformist religion blending materialism and Western vanity with a fraudulently suspicious "church" logo.

El Topo proposes marriage to his mate when he learns that she is pregnant. At the town church, they expect to be married by the priest but El Topo, instead, meets his grown son Brontis. El Topo's son is not monstrous like the townspeople, but Brontis presents a grave threat. Driven by a lifelong hatred of his father, Brontis is prepared to kill El Topo. El Topo persuades his son to postpone the execution until the tunnel is finished. Brontis relents. Months later and the tunnel in operation, the rebellious dwarfs enter the town only to be slaughtered by the malevolent populace wielding guns and rifles. There is nothing rational about the dwarfs storming Main Street in an act of civil disobedience—violence had to be anticipated. The scene has pathos and serves as the film's emotional climax. El Topo is shot during the massacre but he goes on to decimate everyone in the town. In a tragic epilogue, El Topo sets fire to himself, evoking media images of Buddhists self-immolating during the Vietnam War. El Topo's mate goes into labor and she, the infant, and El Topo's grown son ride off into the horizon.

In defense of this film's chaotic narrative, Jodorowsky personalized his feelings and neurosis in nearly every scene and camera shot. Besides carrying the film as the central actor, Jodorowsky wrote the screenplay and film's musical score. When he is successful with a filmic sequence, one sees a prestigious artist working hard to reinvent biblical fables (e.g., Abraham's sacrifice of Isaac) within the myth of the lone Western gunman. The film's unforgettable opening and closing scenes have great visceral command. When Jodorowsky veers off into self-serving vignettes, boundless free association, and forced imagery *El Topo* deteriorates into moments of sophomoric catastrophe. *El Topo* has not been seen by many cult film enthusiasts in part due to difficulty finding the film on VHS and DVD within the United States. The film merits a new generation of film viewers. The written adage as the film begins presents the definition of *El Topo* as a ground mole that uses great determination to climb to the surface only to be blinded by the sun's searing light. Had Jodorowsky stayed focused within his aesthetic cave and avoided some of his campy private jokes and other indulgences, *El Topo* might have achieved cinematic greatness.

Harold and Maude (1971)

The classic notion of December-May relationships usually had one societal interpretation: the old bastard had land, prestige, or untold fortunes. However, in this Hal Ashby film, there is no old bastard. Instead we are given the indomitable aplomb and charming anarchism of Ruth Gordon as the spry, seventy nine year old Maude. She can swipe a highway patrolman's motorcycle faster than a speeding rocket. Her optimism knows no bounds. Her smile is a force of nature. Maude is a tremendous agent of liberation and the personification of Eros to twenty year old Harold Chasen. How could this possibly happen? How could this not happen?

To further the subversive inversion of the December-May model, *Harold and Maude* depicts the younger lover as the grandly rich one. It is Harold who is fixated on death, fatalism, and the suffocating limits of one's choices. He spends his free time staging "theatrical suicides" to annoy his mother. Maude, on the

other hand, sees only the fullness of life and all the sweet possibilities of immediacy, intuition, and improvisation. We sense that Maude has no money nor
need for it. There will be no children from their romantic union, unlike the remarkable possibilities found in traditional December-May matches (e.g., Senator
Strom Thurmond and actor Tony Randall with their young brides). Neither Harold nor Maude has any friends, but instantly they share a very dry, private sense
of humor. He drives a stylized roadster hearse. She drives anything she can steal.
They met by chance at a funeral. Yes, they crash burial services. Their budding
affair is a new variation from the counterculture. The Oedipal complex is cited
briefly in the film, principally as a throwaway joke. Hip viewers sense that this
twenty year old is not dating his grandmother. On the contrary, the laconic,
inscrutable Harold found someone much younger in spirit than he could ever
be—a far cry from his youthful "deadpan" to a geriatric "bedpan."

Mrs. Chasen, Harold's awful mother (Vivian Pickles), has her own materia-
listic agenda. She is one of the movie's several oppressive characters who demand that Harold conform to society. Curiously, Harold's father is absent from
the story. Harold's Uncle Victor (missing a limb) was once General MacAr-
thur's right-hand man. Victor serves up absurd dollops of racism and jingoism in
a misguided portrait of American manhood. Victor's army office wall has a
striking image of Richard Nixon. In the film's satirical view, Victor's line of
reasoning is no crazier than that of the occupant of the White House. Both Mrs.
Chasen and Uncle Victor know Harold is facing a critical rite of passage and, by
symbolic extension, Harold's delayed maturation into adulthood will transform
the nation. Despite his class affluence, Harold's social disaffection can be understood quite accurately as a generational condition. It is this point in the Hal
Ashby story that the audience should perceive the inherent fairy tale of *Harold
and Maude*, rather than the literal realism of *Harold and Maude*. Replacing the
romantic silhouette of the courtly Prince, Harold remains isolated, pathological,
and aloof. His enigmatic emotional state shows neither euphoria nor pain. To
quote a lyric from the rock group Pink Floyd, Harold may be "comfortably
numb." If he enjoys shocking young women dispatched by his mother for blind
dates, the pleasure is subterranean. One would think that Mrs. Chasen would
forewarn these unassuming girls about Harold's suicidal antics, but Mrs. Chasen's inconsiderate error assists the comic plotting.

After two cemetery meetings, Harold and Maude spend a considerable time
together, playfully, generating his new outlook on life. She inspires him to sing,
dance, and laugh. Maude buys him a banjo. They share a peculiar sense of humor. Suddenly, the morose, young man is happier, resolved, and unchained. To
symbolize this dramatic personal change, the film indulges in an extended epi-
sode involving the freeing of a city tree. It is a belabored "acting out" in the
spirit of many campus pranks, but we intuit this to be an important ritual. Harold
and Maude are performing a mating dance of sorts. "I like to watch things
grow," Maude tells him after replanting the tree in a forest, yet she is also refe-
rencing Harold's blossoming.

The blind dates contrived by Harold's mother to produce a marriage are
randomly chosen by computer. The comic film sequence of failed meetings

forecasts the contemporary convention of "speed dating" in churches and synagogues. It is significant to note how Harold's perverse creativity manifests itself with each violent stunt. To Sunshine, he sets himself on fire. To Candy, he lops off a hand (a nod to Uncle Victor?). To Edith, Harold stages an elaborate act of hara-kiri and to our surprise Edith applauds the highly focused performance. In an ingenious reversal, we learn that Edith has some acting experience and that she "gets" Harold. Still, Edith is no closer to Mrs. Chasen's son than any other arranged dates. Harold's mother, thwarted beyond her limits and all patience, pushes her son into military enlistment. Harold helped by Maude outmaneuvers Mrs. Chasen and Uncle Victor with an elaborate staged murder (Harold drowning Maude) which guaranteed Harold's mental and moral unfitness for the armed services.

High school suicide became pandemic in the 1980s and 1990s, generating several thematic black comedy films such as *Heathers* (1989) and *The Virgin Suicides* (1999). There is even a scene in *Heathers* that pays homage to *Harold and Maude*'s "death by hanging" pre-credits stunt. The Ashby film anticipated this disturbing teenage trend by at least fifteen years. The film's audience stays on suicide watch for Harold, but ironically the story has Maude taking her life at the height of her relationship with the boy. An obscure background detail to Maude's character can be detected on her wrist—a tattoo number from a concentration camp.[5] Correlations can be drawn between the genocide experienced by Maude thirty years ago and her willful positivism today. In contrast, Harold and his generation (prior to military service) have no genuine connection to mortality; the obsession Harold has with death probably stems from a pampered and sheltered existence. Because of the upbeat, fable nature of *Harold and Maude*, Ashby and screenwriter Colin Higgins were wise to understate Maude's personal history.

Inevitably and inexorably, the December-May relationship must be consummated; the director handled this taboo tastefully. Harold and Maude confess their love for one another and then proceed to make love in her converted railroad car home. The director cuts away, allowing us to see the post-coital afterglow (blowing bubbles replaced smoking tobacco). We assume that Harold has lost his virginity. What we don't know yet is Maude's firm exit plan. Maude mourns for her dead husband. Perhaps he was lost to the Nazis and life without him has caused her considerable injury. Harold does not pry; the matter stays far in the periphery.

Ashby presents various ineffectual male authority figures, besides mad Uncle Victor, for Harold. Harold's priest instructs the boy on strict morals, outraged by the idea of Harold and Maude fornicating. Harold's psychiatrist indelicately approaches Harold by way of Sigmund Freud. Naturally, all the conformist dogmas miss their audience with Harold Chasen.

Because of the film's fairy tale determinism, Maude's suicide cannot be delayed or cancelled. Her vow to herself over the years is indelible. She was determined to live a good life after surviving her husband. Reaching her eightieth birthday equaled a one way trip up Mount Everest. Maude has seen so many things both good and evil. Satiated and secure, she is prepared to leave the world from this vista. Moreover, she believes that Harold will move on to loving other individuals. Harold's powerful love for her doesn't dissuade Maude's final act. To Maude, her young lover has transformed from catepiller to butterfly. Paradoxically, Harold feels cheated by fate and by Maude directly. *Harold and Maude* is an idealized romance about impermanent love. Judging from life insurance actuary tables, Harold was favored to survive Maude but his senior lover hastened that inevitability.

The extraordinary good feelings that were sparked by this endearing movie trailed actor Ruth Gordon until her death 1985: "I can walk down the streets of any city, including Edgartown on Martha's Vineyard, and people hand me oat straw tea, boxes of chocolates, photos of their city, and daisies" (Daisies and oat straw tea are signature items in *Harold and Maude).*[6]

Harold and Maude began as a twenty minute student film by Colin Higgins at UCLA. Paramount Pictures took on the project and Higgins expanded the script to ninety minutes.[7] The film encountered great trouble at the box office even with the studio's pragmatic expectations. Paramount was nervous about the film's survival when early reports disparaged the film for its perverse storyline. The entire producing team knew the film was a self-styled black comedy. Despite a disappointing release, the film enjoyed a miraculous second life on college campuses and became a runaway cult hit breaking major city attendance records. College students were wild about *Harold and Maude*—the quintessential date movie for the 1970s. Straw polls list the film as the cult favorite according to National Public Radio essayist Soren McCarthy.[8] Paramount, now properly clued in, mounted a more successful re-release campaign, hitting the youth market squarely on and off campus. Contributing significantly to the overall sound and feel of the movie is the buoyant, folk rock music of Cat Stevens (now Yusaf Islam). The songs work often to contrast Ashby's ironic distancing. Stevens' sensitive compositions and lyrics link all the film's sequences seamlessly, adding music-video flair a decade before the reign of MTV.

The Wicker Man (1973)

The remote Hebridean island community within this film that conspires against a British police officer has several attributes that defy, disturb, and beguile. An esoteric faith rules the region and the islanders are well prepared to engineer an elaborate and fatal parlor game at the expense of Sergeant Neil Howie. It is not enough to state that the denizens of Summerisle are connivers empowered by a powerfully old religion, uninhibited sexual permissiveness, and a charismatic Lord Summerisle. They are unified in their veiled mission for collective survival. Even the Hebridean children are part of the staged lie. When the film audience catches on to the deception, there is a concrete sense of dread and nausea. It is that paralyzing dread that will overwhelm the British victim at his most vulnerable hour of life. Adding to the theatrical impact of *The Wicker Man*, our identification with Sergeant Howie (sterling Edward Woodward) is quite intense and personal. His manly innocence comes not from naiveté. His reckoning has immense pathos. His demise echoes a dark fable from the Old Testament. His reward for maintaining his virginity is a death sentence. Such is the inversion of the values of punishment and reward. *The Wicker Man* blends the popular genres of horror and detective story into a most peculiar concoction. Certainly, the weird flushes of humor found within this film are exquisitely conceived. After all, the maniacal Summerisle folks at first glance show the sergeant only the cheery "travel poster" side of village life.

This wonderfully strange British movie continues to astound new generations of cult audiences, particularly after an extremely clumsy remake in 2006 by the American playwright Neil LaBute. The story straddles two mystery genres—plots about witchcraft and thrillers featuring an urbanite victimized by rural conspirators.[9] Presented is a morose tale that calls into question how a virtuous man of stern Christian faith, who demands nothing more than to serve his society and fight wrongdoing, can suffer beyond all reason and proportion. Director Robin Hardy displayed an uncanny instinct for making the macabre in rural nature appear utterly wholesome and quaint. Working in tandem with a mystery genre playwright noted for his West End smash hit *Sleuth*, Anthony Shaffer, the creative team behind *The Wicker Man* unearths a staged reality that feels often as convincing as an anthropological documentary by the BBC. This Scottish community is so thoroughly devoted to paganism and human sacrifice that, from an academic vantage, it would be revolutionary to suspend judgment on the climatic murderous act. Hardy and Shaffer deliver a riveting interpretation of pantheist life and moral relativism. The Celtic context for *The Wicker Man* can trace its lineage back to the practice of human sacrifice by pre-Christian pagans of the British Isles. Moreover, in Sir James Fraiser's *The Golden Bough*, various human sacrifices had occurred within large burning wicker effigies in Europe. Within the English occult film tradition, several tropes are delineated with regard to the renegade magician, the female witch, and the ongoing battle between old and new religion—which is to say the resurgence of paganism in the modern world.[10]

The first cleverly deceptive touch to this film is the note of thanks before the credits begin from the filmmakers to Lord Summerisle and the residents of Summerisle for permitting them the freedom to record their religious rites and practices. The statement creates an expectation of a docu-drama.

The overriding strategy to this film brings an ironic chord of Sophocles to contemporary audiences. The central character, *The Wicker Man,* is as unknowing as Oedipus, while the surrounding dramatic participants see the meticulous arrangement of their respective assignments and the inevitability of the protagonist to fall.

Sent to the West Highlands Constabulary is an unsigned note and child's photo prompting the authorities to visit Summerisle to investigate the missing Rowan Morrison. Flying to the remote Hebridean island, Sergeant Howie is unescorted on this mission. Once he leaves the small commuter plane, he is completely on his own.

The inhabitants regard him with pointed suspicion and deny any knowledge that a little girl has disappeared. The sergeant is determined to see through this charade. Even the presumed mother of Rowan, May Morrison, says nothing to Howie to dissuade him. May's daughter, Myrtle, shocks the sergeant, saying she has a hand drawing of Rowan. Her Rowan is a little rabbit.

Howie lodges in the pub owned by Alder MacGregor. MacGregor's sexually alluring daughter Willow (Britt Ekland) signals her availability to the sergeant and provides him with one of several spiritual tests. The randy songs at the pub unsettle Howie. He witnesses naked lovemaking by many in the town cemetery. At the school Howie finds the teacher informing girls about phallic magic. Outside the boys indulge themselves in a sexualized maypole rite. No one at school verifies Rowan's existence, but the sergeant spots her name on the office register. The teacher tries to assuage Howie with the privileged news that Rowan has died and continues to live within another life form.

Doggedly, Howie discovers Rowan's tombstone. He engages Lord Summerisle in a lengthy discussion about the perverse elements of the pagan islanders. Lord Summerisle identifies the community's concern about the crop failure this year as their crucible. The sergeant states his belief that Rowan was murdered and that many people are covering up the truth. Howie requests permission to unearth the girl's coffin. Lord Summerisle extends full courtesy to the sergeant. When Howie opens the coffin, inside is a rabbit's corpse. The ensuing mystery becomes clear to the appalled British police officer. Rowan Morrison is alive and has been designated for a ritualistic sacrifice as May Day approaches. From this point forward, Howie must cease his survey and take direct action.

On May Day, the sergeant overcomes MacGregor and assumes MacGregor's village idiot costume. Howie takes his place in the May Day processional as it wends its way to the beautiful, austere shoreline. The crowd sequence moving to the film's climax has bits of pandemonium and pageantry. Rowan is spotted by Howie and he tries to free her. Howie is captured while the revelers sing. Lord Summerisle informs the sergeant that his sacrifice will be potent in light of Howie's virginity, his authority as a member of Her Majesty's rule, and to his journey to Summerisle at this precise moment of sacrifice.

Howie, bound and sentenced, finds himself with other sacrificial animals inside the torso of a gigantic wicker armature silhouetting a primitive man. The people of Summerisle surround the scorching figure while voicing the Middle English folksong "*Sumer Is Icumen In.*" Howie, left with his solitary faith, sings out Psalm 23.

From a cult films perspective, *The Wicker Man* has many similarly arresting themes and narrative devices found in *Rosemary's Baby* (1968). Both stories require an unsuspecting protagonist to play a central role in an intricately covert (dare one say cultist?) plot. Both feature the harsh clash of cultural and religious beliefs when it becomes clear to the protagonist that something horribly out of the ordinary is happening. Both press the protagonist to the threshold of utter isolation and madness. Both end with the triumph of anti-Christian groups that could well scare a mainstream film audience. Both show that hidden skillfully within our society are communities that can masquerade, fooling us about their beliefs and hidden agendas. Both, in the baldest sense, depict the raw battle between good and evil. Together, they build a strong case about respectable identity and the inversion of identity, which is another way to describe the capacity of the dark "Other" seen by ourselves in a metaphysical mirror. Critic Danny Peary compared *The Wicker Man* to *Horror Hotel* (1960)—a film that showed a student, lured to a Massachusetts town, who is sacrificed by acts of witchcraft.[11] More recently, the theme is revisited in *The Skeleton Key* (2005) as a young hospital aide is tricked and defeated by sorcerers and voodoo.

While it is true that the majority of western horror movies rely on the power of Christianity to thwart the darker forces of life, films like *The Exorcist* (1973), *The Omen* (1976), and *The Ring* (2002) declare another philosophical sensibility that is full of disquietude and fear. *The Wicker Man* is inconclusive about the victory by Lord Summerisle and his followers, while *Rosemary's Baby* (1968) ends with the victorious birth of the antichrist. We do not know if the island in *The Wicker Man* will be blessed with crops for the following year. However, the consequences of the Summerisle beliefs are immaterial to the effectiveness of Summerisle's machinations given the ritualism. We might assume, too, that the British authorities will never discover how Sergeant Howie vanished which adds another note of silent alarm to the movie audience.

Actor Christopher Lee was famous for playing Dracula in a British series of mid-century horror classics. The chance to enlarge his repertoire with the role of Lord Summerisle motivated Lee to sign on early with Robin Hardy and Anthony Shaffer. Although Lee was extremely proud of his work in *The Wicker Man*, much of his acting was trimmed out of the film as it went from 102 minutes to 87 minutes.[12] Screenwriter Shaffer delved into an exhaustive investigation of pagan life in preparation for the original script. The production company British Lion was sold during the film's postproduction. *The Wicker Man* suffered a chain of bad breaks in reaching distribution and was very nearly shelved. Thanks to Roger Corman's New World Pictures, a finished print of the film was secured mysteriously even though Corman had no hand in actual distribution.

Finally, the annual Burning Man event in America's southwest desert is often cited as a ceremonial homage to Robin Hardy's film. According to the official Burning Man website, there is no conscious connection between the film and Burning Man founder Larry Harvey.

Notes:

1   J. Hoberman and Jonathan Rosenbaum, *Midnight Movies* (New York: Da Capo Press, 1983), 88.

2   Hoberman and Rosenbaum, *Midnight Movies*, 93-94.

3   Hoberman and Rosenbaum, *Midnight Movies*, 95.

4   Danny Peary, *Cult Movies* (New York: Dell, 1981), 76-77.

5   Peary, *Cult Movies*, 138.

6   J. Hoberman and Jonathan Rosenbaum, *Midnight Movies* (New York: Da Capo Press, 1983), 298.

7   Danny Peary, *Cult Movies* (New York: Dell, 1981), 136.

8   Soren McCarthy, *Cult Movies in Sixty Seconds* (London: Fusion Press, 2003), 96.

9   Karl French and Philip French, *Cult Movies* (New York: Billboard Books, 2000), 226.

10   Leon, Hunt, *Necromancy in the U.K.: Witchcraft and the Occult in British Horror*; Steve Chibnall, ed., *British Horror Cinema* (London and New York: Routledge, 2002), 85.

11   Danny Peary, *Cult Movies* (New York: Dell, 198), 165.

12   Peary, *Cult Movies*, 165.

Chapter Seven
Films from the 1980s

Taking a page from Oliver Stone's film *Wall Street* (1987), in which the audacious capitalist Gordon Gekko pronounces to a stockholder's meeting that "greed is good," Tom Wolfe's satirical novel, *Bonfire of the Vanities* (1987) probes the greed and self-interest of New York City's corporate elite. In the ascendancy of Ronald Reagan's conservative revolution, the nation readjusted to a view of entitlement and largess in all areas of life. Clearly, Reagan's charisma and ease with public discourse helped spread the philosophy of his optimism about America's economic and cultural greatness. Amazingly, the Berlin Wall came down in 1989 and Germany was reunified. In the final leg of the Cold War, Reagan believed that our nation would outspend the Russians in a 'Star Wars' missile defense shield. The matter of the efficacy of the missile system was almost beside the point. The antipathy toward Communist insurgencies steered American attention to Nicaragua and the Contras' covert operations. At the start of his presidency, Reagan challenged the air traffic controllers union PATCO and fired the striking employees. The nation's unemployment rate hovered precipitously high at the 10% mark. In 1983 the president endorsed the invasion of Grenada and Reagan endured in the same year the Arab bombing of an American base in Beirut that resulted in the death of 243 marines. The initial appearance of the AIDS epidemic swept forcefully into the 1980s, first as a mysterious illness and later as a political controversy in light of the federal government's sluggish response. A further blight impacted the nation as crack cocaine's popularity went unchallenged for years. Echoing the power of the assassin as experienced in the 1960s, the world was stunned by the attempted murders of Ronald Reagan and Pope John Paul II in 1981. Ex-Beatle John Lennon was murdered in 1980. Fittingly, the decade witnessed a surge in working class film heroes of the likes of Rambo in *First Blood* (1982, the sequel in 1985) and in 1988, *Die Hard's* John McClane. The nightmarish *Fatal Attraction* (1987) mesmerized the American public, depicting a vilified lover involved with a "blameless" married man. Oprah Winfrey introduced a new tone to daytime television that shattered what was once taboo on topic and theme, and comedian Bill Cosby redefined the upper-middle class American family with his smash African American situation comedy. Disney Studios had tremendous insight and luck in the release of *The Little Mermaid* (1989), which chartered an ingenious course for musical feature film animation. With trends in technology colliding, home video recording systems fought for dominance and VHS defeated Sony's Betamax format. A new culture of video rental stores and home viewing arose. Video games, too, exploded in acceptance and variation. Certainly, the most impressive innovation of the decade was the home computer and the immediacy of the computer's influence in all aspects of business and personal needs. Toni

Morrison, Don DeLillo, John Irving, Cynthia Ozick, Carl Sagan, Allan Bloom, John Guare, David Mamet, Wendy Wasserstein, and William Kennedy are some of the authors that gave distinction to the period. Michael Jackson became the king of pop music. Whitney Houston, Billy Joel, Stevie Wonder, Bruce Springsteen, Prince, Madonna, and super groups such as U2 enjoyed rock's top tier as LP records were phased out and CDs entered the market. MTV reigned thoroughly through the decade and music production invariably meant video accompaniment. Despite the authoritative stewardship of Ronald Reagan and the media's embrace of his presidency, the tragic space shuttle Challenger disaster in 1986 had cast a formidable pall on the nation.

Road Warrior (1981)

Within the span of sixteen years, Australian film director George Miller has earned the fine distinction of authoring two contemporary screen classics, diametrically opposite in theme and sensibility, which generated successful, much discussed sequels. The accomplishment is not taken lightly by a good many film critics. Film fans were quietly astonished to discover Miller's screenplay *Babe* (1995), an animal film fable with pungent Hobbesian overtones for children, seen in context with Miller's wild motorcycle film for action-genre adults—*Mad Max* (1979). Miller's aesthetic split personality, as it were, seemed to prefigure Steven Spielberg's *E.T./Schindler's List* dichotomy.

Set in the near future, *Mad Max*—the first of the *Mad Max* film trilogy—has a very young and pliant Mel Gibson portraying the tired, embittered cop Max Rockatansky (Max's irregular surname is perhaps a cult film trivia treasure). Miller's seriousnesness is genuine and the heart of the film concerns Max seeking revenge for the wanton death of his wife and son. On the other hand, *Babe*, featuring a talking piglet, approaches the notion of mortality and family ties from a different angle altogether. Both stark tales from Miller identify the universal risks in life on a Darwinian planet and, with these powerful risks, the need to find absolute self-reliance.

Mad Max was George Miller's first feature film direction and at the time there was no expectation that the low budget project would have any traction in world cinema and in the essays of cultural critics. But immediately, the iconic character and compromised heroism of Max found an adoring audience beyond Australia and grindhouse theatres. Of cultural note, *Mad Max* did far better than *Star Wars* in the Australian market.[1] The thin transparency of the *Mad Max*'s vengeance motif brings to mind Charles Bronson's vigilante urban nightmare, *Deathwish* (1974), by director Michael Winner, while the Australian outback provides Miller ample frontier and existential space to evoke classic John Ford westerns.

The Miller story—*Road Warrior*—co-written by Terry Hayes and Brian Hannant, is set in a bleak, dyspeptic post-apocalyptic desert where anarchy is ever-present and marauding gangs do anything for a vital liter of gasoline or an easy kill. Killing appears to be one of the few remaining pleasures in Miller's fantasia. The film is in love with a future "antiquity" littered by semi-trailer wrecks, modified motorcycles, stripped autos, and badly broken oil tankers. The mythologized car by Miller and his production team enhanced the fetishistic exploration by fellow Australian director Peter Weir in his debut film, *The Cars That Ate Paris* (1974).[2] Spoken language is a spare as the diesel fuel, and what is said remains free of any verbal flourishes or tossed off wisecracks. Further, while *Mad Max* was a product of overdubbing to correct Australian accents, *Road Warrior* (originally titled *Mad Max 2*) allowed original voices to remain, including Mel Gibson's.[3] The extremity of the film's bizarre visual style, ritualistic conceits, and amoral compass evokes another landscape of vintage decadence, Fellini's *Satyricon* (1969). Watching the well executed action sequences mounting climactically is hypnotic and addictive. Cinematographer Dean Semier and his team, assisted by expert editing, have assembled high octane chases, collisions, and breathtaking stunts shot by cameras within the vehicles.

Road Warrior begins with a narrator's memory of world war that destroyed modern civilization. The identity of the narrator becomes the final twist in the movie. The stolid manner of the prologue at first appears heavy-handed and too functional—like a 1940s newsreel without a hint of any irony. The narrator, who sounds old and exhausted with life, introduces Max as a man who had suffered a personal tragedy prior to the global horror. Max's only companion is a faithful Australian cattle dog (or more precisely a Blue Heeler). Max has a run-in with a gang of marauders and then a Bruegelesque helicopter pilot, Gyro Captain, who has to bargain for his life and reluctantly informs Max about a major gasoline compound. Perched like vultures just outside the compound, the gang of marauders has made camp, and these thugs are under the iron fist rule of a masked man, Humongous. Critical to the storyboarding, Max, in expectation of a large gasoline payment, assists an injured member of the compound past the nihilistic gang. The compound is surprised by Max's entrance and horrified that the man transported by Max has died in transit. The tribal leader of the compound, Pappagallo (father chicken in Spanish) denies honoring the fuel payment to Max. Within the compound a wordless waif, Feral Kid, who can kill with his sharpened boomerang, gravitates to Max while the small community disdains Max. The boy's attraction to Max has significance in light of Max's murdered son. Pappagallo propositions Max to drive the compound's tanker truck full of fuel past the marauders and safely to a paradise within a day's drive.

Max senses that the proposed mission would be suicide and leaves the compound with just his dog. Immediately, Max is pummeled by the marauders and Max's car is destroyed. The Australian cattle dog is murdered and Gyro Captain flies in to save a bloodied Max. Now Max rethinks the compound's proposal about the tanker trunk and has to convince Pappagallo that he is still strong enough to accomplish the task. The climax requires Max to commandeer the tanker while the compound members stealthily take flight in a separate direction. Feral Kid jumps into the tanker cabin and a few heroic compound fighters aid Max. Gyro Captain hovers overhead during a kinetic chase and demolition derby. After a series of intense killings, Max and a handful of gangsters realize that the tanker truck was a decoy carrying sand and not a drop of gasoline. Apparently, the compound's bet paid off and the dwellers had ably smuggled out the fuel in their separate vehicles.

Feral Kid, according to the unseen narrator, joins the community exodus as they journey north with their new unlikely chief, Gyro Captain. For a fleeting moment, one might discern the spiritual connection between Max and the lost feral boy. In another generation to come, Feral Kid becomes the Great Northern Tribe's leader and Feral Kid identifies himself as the narrator. With this coda, we get the sense that civilization is building itself out of this nuclear oblivion and yet we lose all story ties to Max. Taking into account all three Mad Max films, including *Mad Max Beyond Thunderdome* (1985), a pronounced childlike motif adds dimensionality and brings biblical overtones to the saga.[4]

As in earlier allegorical desert films like *El Topo* (1971) and *The Good, the Bad and the Ugly* (1966), the laconic character of Max is in keeping as the friendless hero and an anomaly with a veiled past, insufficient future, and momentary present grace. The mystique that propels Max into cult status has much to do with the distressed motorcycle leathers that comprise his outfitting and the unsentimental destiny that faces Max at each plot point. Certainly, Max is more than a fashion statement and yet his black wardrobe is in keeping with his pessimistic, outsider stature. His evil counterpart in the film, Wez, also sports an outstanding leather costume (with feathers) exposing more skin than Max and, with each sequence, Wez's appearance takes on an overture of sexual violence and references the trendiness of nihilistic aggressive dress in punk subculture in major cities such as London, New York, and Berlin.[5]

According to AOL Moviefone Cinematical and other electronic entertainment news sources, George Miller—fresh after his *Happy Feet* family animation Oscar in 2007—is going ahead with *Mad Max 4*, but he will not be tapping iconoclastic Mel Gibson for the role.

Blade Runner (1982)

Of all the cyberspace-themed authors emerging on the national scene in the 1980s, William Gibson and Philip K. Dick were foremost in the limelight. The two visionaries shared sociological and political concerns verging on a paranoiac edge. While Gibson continues to write, Dick died the year that *Blade Runner* was released by Warner Brothers. Dick never saw the completed version of director Ridley Scott's ambitious interpretation of Dick's *Do Androids Dream of Electric Sheep*, but the novelist did manage to see some daily outtakes and industry word had it that Dick was not entirely unhappy with the celluloid outcome.[6] Regrettably, Scott's ambitious film failed with most of the critics and could not find an American fan base for box office acceptance. The film performed more satisfactorily in foreign markets. Like many intelligent science fiction films (e.g., *Thx 1138* [1971] by George Lucas and *The Man Who Fell to Earth* [1976] by Nicolas Roeg), *Blade Runner*'s importance grew powerfully in subsequent decades in comparable fashion to Philip K. Dick's climb in serious literary circles here and abroad. Clearly, film director and novelist were ahead of their time and the respective artists were braced for considerable popular misunderstanding. The studio forced Ridley Scott to include a "gumshoe detective" narration by Harrison Ford in order to facilitate the comprehension of Ford's opaque protagonist. The director's cut DVD version omits the narration and enriched the cult audience for the film.[7]

Foreshadowing cyberpunk sub-genre, Philip K. Dick depicted the jaded elements of California life, alienation, and authoritative oppression. Ridley Scott proved a magnificently matched collaborator to embroider Dick's idiosyncratic detachment to heroic contemporary fiction. Recurrent ideas in all of Dick's fascinating stories expressed his fears of being real and safe in a universe that held no welcome for intelligent paranoids. He reinterpreted humanism in a postmodern prism of thought and application.[8] Dick became the first science fiction author to be honored in the prestigious Library of America series featuring luminaries Saul Bellow, John Steinbeck, and William Faulkner. For director Ridley Scott, the professional title for these bounty hunters compelled him to rename the film to boost the poetic conceit of the story. Helped by his co-screenwriter Hampton Fancher, Scott gravitated to the Alan E. Nourse novel *The Bladerunner* (1974)—about people who take medical equipment to outlaw physicians. What first served as a working title for the project became the final tag, even after Fancher left the collaboration. Screenwriter David Peoples then came aboard.

Blade Runner presents a post-nuclear war Los Angeles in 2019 and a lone figure named Rick Deckard. In Dick's book, Deckard is a well established bounty hunter who is married to a miserable individual. Deckard observes a religion called Mercerism and pops stimulants to improve his dour mood. In his dreams, Deckard envisions that he has a real animal to own and love. In 2019, innumerable artificial animals and androids assume many of the working roles once given to humans. Deckard tracks these 'replicants' that are indistinguishable from humans. Common to the novel and to the film, these androids are clever, heartless, and altogether evil. The novel's romantic lead, Rachel, has more delicacy and empathy than her colleague androids. Still, she has a menacing side and has no compunction about destroying Deckard's pet goat.

In Scott's film, Rachel fulfils a necessary Hollywood archetype for the idealized love object. Unlike her book's counterpart, Rachel harms no living being. Played with conviction by Sean Young, Rachel is as innocent and adorable as a fairy tale ingénue. She appeals to Deckard (Harrison Ford) so completely that he lets down his guard and his attraction to her suggests a new idea about miscegenation in America. More significantly, the novel does not stress the androids' motivation to lobby the android manufacturer to prolong their shelf life on earth. This plot point is critical to *Blade Runner*. Dick's story reveals that Mercerism is fraudulent, the police force is comprised of androids, and that Deckard suspects that he might not be human.[9] These vital points have no bearing in Scott's movie and yet *Blade Runner* yields unforgettable dramatic philosophy and emotional residue in support of Philip K. Dick's obsessions.

Assisted by conceptual artist Syd Mead and designer Lawrence G. Paull, Scott composed a film that encapsulates urban America's next cancerous horizon. We see in the opening sequence vibrant neon advertising for Coca-Cola, TDK and RCA over a swatch of imposing factory chimneys. The belching fires and black smoke suggest a post-technological Hieronymus Bosch landscape in the bowels of hell. The modern engineering combines retrofitted utilization and inhuman machinery. The broad innovation to this architectural society in 2019 is not found in new prototypes but rather randomly in the add-on supplements as awful as plumbing parts, window trims, and displaced car mufflers. The notion is paradoxical in light of the age's accelerated production of hard-to-detect androids. Humankind's progress could not be more dystopic and endangered. Scott's uncompromising rendering is the antithesis of the Age of Enlightenment.

Blade Runner identifies Tyrell, the CEO manufacturer of replicants, as the mastermind of this malignancy. This is perhaps an advance from '60s and '70s paranoia films that could not name the corporate seat of power.[10] Tyrell could have abandoned earth for a paradise outside the planet, but he is determined to populate replicant slaves for domestic productivity. Tyrell cannot extract himself from the genetic engineering system he has perfected and come to love. The class domination theme, as handled by Scott, provides a sharp reminder of Fritz Lang's *Metropolis*.

Four Nexus 6 replicants have journeyed back to earth in the hope of countermanding their respective termination dates. They have killed almost two dozen humans and there is little time remaining. One Tyrell Corporation employee, Leon, undergoes a Voight-Kampff probe with prompts that challenge a subject's emotional composition. The officiating Tyrell agent, Holden, chips away with questions about Leon's mother. For a moment we sympathize with the employee. Leon fails the empathy test and murders the agent.

Enter Rick Deckard, who is ordered back into duty by Tyrell. At the corporation, Tyrell official Bryant briefs him on the at-large replicants. The sleek, lead rebel is Roy Batty. Leon Kowalski is the ordinary looking, proletariat-worker. Zhora is designed for martial arts assassination. Erotically beautiful Pris is geared for pure physical pleasure. Deckard will team up with Gaff, another Blade Runner. In his session at the corporation, Bryant sets up another psychological probe on Tyrell's executive assistant Rachael, with Deckard participating.

Deckard is intrigued by her despite knowing that she is replicant filled with false memories and enhanced human vulnerability. With Rachael's manifestation, Tyrell has achieved something new in android technology. The understated exchange between Deckard and Rachael serves an intense and poetic counterpoint to the previous Voight-Kampff test. It is as though a psychic connection between human and android were forged that will forever change Deckard's outlook. To make matters more complex for Deckard, he witnesses in Bryant's presence Rachael confronting her self-illusion about being human.

Deckard and Gaff search Leon's apartment while Roy and Leon hunt key members of the Corporation, beginning with the Tyrell eye designer. The replicants expect to work their way up the ladder from the eye designer to Sebastian, and eventually to Tyrell himself. Rachael surprises Deckard at his home. Her hope is to convince Deckard of her humanity and her practical innocence. On a hunch, Deckard tracks Zhora to a smutty strip joint. Zhora, in the guise of a semi-naked snake dancer, nearly overpowers Deckard during a wild chase through dense street traffic and as she flees, Deckard takes her out with his gun. Soon afterward, Deckard sees Bryant again and Deckard is informed that Rachael has fled the Tyrell office. As a result, Bryant demands that Deckard add her to the list of android terminations.

Obligating Deckard, Rachael saves him from Leon's assault. At this moment in the story, Deckard and Rachael have fallen for each other. Deckard's professionalism is severely compromised. Elsewhere in Los Angeles, Pris and Roy have coerced Tyrell's Sebastian to help the replicants reach Tyrell. The action turns to Tyrell's penthouse. Roy Batty requires Tyrell to extend the replicants' lifespan and extracts a promise from him not to hunt the replicants down in the future. With Tyrell not cooperating, Roy murders Tyrell and Sebastian.

Deckard is surprised by Pris within Sebastian's apartment. The dangerous confrontation leads to Pris' termination just as Roy enters. Roy toys with Deckard within the apartment building and onto the roof. Clearly, Roy has the superior edge over this Blade Runner. Hanging from the roof beam, Deckard assumes that his death is imminent. However, Roy reaches down for Deckard and extends unexpected generosity. For Roy Batty, his four year android lifespan coming to an end, he has a genuine epiphany about humanity and his own transcendence. Moments later, Roy expires and the film audience must realign its judgment of these brutal androids.

Deckard goes home and discovers Rachael waiting. They know what has transpired and what lies ahead. Deckard's partner Graff has left him a paper-fold unicorn—Graff's calling card. But certainly the origami represents the fragility of a forbidden romantic union, for Deckard and Rachel have won each other in a world without hopeful destiny.

Blue Velvet (1986)

Artist David Lynch had stunned experienced elite cult and midnight audiences with his groundbreaking, surrealistically bleak, black and white film, *Eraserhead* (1977) and had generated a second impressive tidal wave with audiences and critics on the premiere of *Blue Velvet* (1986). The artistic impact from Lynch's Reagan era film was impossible to ignore. What Lynch did to a mainstream Hollywood studio film demonstrated subversive independence and solipsistic brilliance on par with *Freaks* in the 1930s and *Psycho* in the 1960s. Lynch personalized violence in a meditative direction even if the outward result in *Blue Velvet* appears more gratuitous than symbolic. The range of top cult directors and films that have been influenced by Lynch's rarefied angst, narrative freedom, and psycho-sexual landscapes stretch from Quentin Tarantino, *Pulp Fiction* (1994) to Christopher Nolan, *Memento* (2000). Indubitably, Lynch's movie was the perfectly vile grenade to throw at Ronald Reagan's nostalgic reinvention of America and at the Republican Party's idealization of small towns and exurbia. According to Lynch, the film took on internal life with Lynch's memories of Bobby Vinton's pop version of the song "Blue Velvet."[11]

Jeffrey Beaumont is a college student summoned home to Lumberton because of his father's hospitalization from a crippling stroke. The duration of Jeffrey's visit is considerable but he is comfortable living at home with his mother and aunt. While working in his father's hardware store, Jeffrey rediscovers the town in a completely new perspective. Walking through an open field from the hospital, he spots a severed human ear. Why an ear (a reference to Van Gogh)? According to Lynch, he wanted a body part with "an opening."[12] This object becomes the first of many puzzle pieces for Jeffrey in his quest to solve a terrifying mystery in Lumberton. Suspecting foul play, Jeffrey contacts the police official Williams. Jeffrey's early involvement with Detective Williams leads to meeting Williams' high school daughter Sandy. She tips off Jeffrey to investigate a woman named Dorothy Vallens—a singer with very shady connections to a mob figure.

Highly motivated, Jeffrey passes himself off as a maintenance worker to fool Dorothy Vallens. He spies her brief encounter with a large man dressed in canary yellow and impulsively swipes a second set of house keys from Vallens. Later that evening, Jeffrey and Sandy catch Dorothy's act at the local club. Critical to Jeffrey's actions and hormones is his compulsion to sneak into the singer's apartment while Sandy waits in the car. He has crossed the line without respect to good judgment, self-control, and safe conduct.

Of course, Jeffrey misses the warning signal from Sandy; Dorothy is about to enter her apartment. He hides inside her closet. Dorothy pulls him out and taunts him with a knife. She then forces sexual contact with Jeffrey. The intrusion takes a turn for the worse with the arrival of the film's psychopathic killer, Frank Booth. Jeffrey returns to his hiding space as Frank terrorizes Dorothy. Frank relies on unbearable violence and a mask inhaler for enhanced sensual climaxes with Dorothy. Clearly, young Jeffrey has seen more mystery than he can tolerate consciously.

Dorothy accepts Jeffrey into her troubled world and she implores him to understand her despite the horrible things Jeffrey witnessed. He learns that Frank has done something to Dorothy's husband and son. Having followed Frank and Frank's associates, including the yellow-jacketed man, Jeffrey also photographs them. Later at police headquarters, Jeffrey identifies yellow-jacketed Gordon as Detective Williams' partner. Williams underplays the significance of the miscellaneous clues about drug crimes and Frank gathered by Jeffrey, but reminds the young man about the perils of mixing with this crowd. In this narrative interval, Jeffrey and Sandy build a personal friendship despite the fact that she already has a boyfriend.

When Jeffrey visits Dorothy a second time, they have sex. Later, Frank catches him exiting the home and forces him into Frank's car. Jeffrey realizes he is in great danger. On a long car drive to a remote section of Lumberton, Frank plays with Jeffrey's nerves. The mobster paints his captive's mouth with lipstick in preparation for an unexpected kiss and devastating brutalizing.

Perhaps Jeffrey has learned his lesson. He resumes with Sandy; they go to a teenage party. When Jeffrey takes Sandy to his home, he is surprised by a battered Dorothy who appears naked on his front porch. Sandy realizes that Jeffrey has been unfaithful and has ventured into a disturbing triangle with Dorothy and Frank. Jeffrey brings Dorothy to the hospital and decides to continue on alone to her apartment. His motivation based on impulse again rather than anything empirical. This might be the last time he risks his life.

Detective Williams stakes out Frank's building while Jeffrey finds the yellow-jacketed man's corpse and Dorothy's dead husband inside her apartment. Yellow-jacketed man's police radio is still operative. Jeffrey is transfixed by the presence of death and he braces for Dorothy's torturer. Frank bursts in. Jeffrey grabs the yellow-jacket's gun and jumps into the closet. Within seconds, Frank discovers his prey's location. As the closet door opens, Jeffrey guns down Frank. Jeffrey has now tasted murder in the exact room where he tasted extreme sexual adventure. His last phase of protracted boyhood has passed as if he were a wretched soldier coming home after war.

Lynch cuts to a buoyant coda in suburban repose. It is a warm, happy day; Jeffrey and Sandy share a meal with family and a peaceful robin is perched on the window sill. A worm is caught in the robin's beak, but the bright sunlight mitigates any discomfort about the bird's meal. Lynch captures the paradox of paradise as the inhabitants of Lumberton cohabitate innocently with the dark spirit of evil. The film viewer can ruminate on the fleeting value of the innocence. In the next frame, we see Dorothy on a park bench, embracing her darling little boy and bidding her nightmare a final goodbye.

Lynch's debts to Alfred Hitchcock are manifold. *Blue Velvet* incorporates a lifelong theme for Hitchcock, namely, the conversion and corruption of an innocent bystander into a mistaken figure caught in a deadly crossfire between civil authorities and cunning evil forces. Fetishes and sexual prohibitions found in many Hitchcock films have resurfaced with stylish conceits in Lynch's realm. Voyeurism experienced in Hitchcock's *Rear Window* (1954), *Vertigo* (1958), and *Psycho* (1960) envelops the character Jeffrey into same psychological fold, as Jeffrey discovers his hidden self while trapped inside Dorothy's closet. Intimate contact between sexual abandon and death are common to Hitchcock's and Lynch's personalized cinema.

Composer Angelo Badalamenti has collaborated on many leading Lynch projects including the highly praised cult television series, *Twin Peaks* (1990-91). Badalamenti's moody, addictive, and sensual tapestries enrich *Blue Velvet* in untold ways and as powerfully as Bernard Hermann assisted Hitchcock. Badalamenti's mesmerizing music offsets the cascading visual violence with a disassociated haze to the senses and a memorable opiate for the mind long after the movie ends.

Lynch had offered that much of the film's ending came from his dreams (e.g., the police radio sound, Frank's disguise, the gun in the yellow jacket's pocket).[13] He also had stated in various interviews that *Eraserhead* articulated his fears of fatherhood and sustained romantic intimacy. *Blue Velvet* does not exactly contradict that articulation, but one can interpret the positive turn in Dorothy's world as an affirmation about parenting and spiritual redemption.[14] Similarly, Jeffrey's return to Sandy gives promise to the possibilities of bobby sox love to us all, thirty years after Elvis and Bobby Vinton first sang to America.

The legion of Lynch detractors likes to devalue his work as self-indulgent, incoherent, malevolent, misogynistic, contemptuous, and pornographic. Despite his fortuitous debut on network television with *Twin Peaks* (1990-1991), his screen work after 1986 has not equaled the command, vehemence, and vision of *Blue Velvet*, which must be called his premiere masterpiece and one of the most influential American films of the last thirty years. He picked up younger audiences with *Lost Highway* (1997) and *Mulholland Drive* (2001), but these latter films paled in scope and intensity. It has to be noted, too, that many film fans adore Lynch's elegant and clear-sighted Victorian biography of deformed Joseph Merrick's *Elephant Man* (1980), perhaps as many who have reviled his one major backfire, *Dune* (1984)—an adaptation of Frank Herbert's science fiction epic. As eerie and transcendental as Lynch's films are, there is nothing more bizarre than identifying the respective producers for *Elephant Man* and *Dune*, farceur Mel Brooks and Italian mogul Dino De Laurentiis.

The invitation to impersonate and caricaturize auteur David Lynch, tieless and austere, in his elegant formal suit and a coiffure of sterling gray hair inspired comedian Martin Short to the debauched task in Short's *Jiminy Glick in Lala Wood* (2005), and with this madcap tribute came Short's bald parody of opening and closing scenes of *Lost Highway*.

Notes:

1   Jerome Shapiro, *Atomic Bomb Cinema: The Apocalyptic Imagination on Film* (New York and London: Routledge, 2002), 173.

2   Xavier Mendik and Graeme Harper, eds., *Unruly Pleasures: The Cult Film and its Critics*; Jonathan Rayner, *The Cult Film, Roger Corman and The Cars That Ate Paris* (Guildford: FAB Press, 2000), 230.

3   Danny Peary, *Cult Movies 3* (New York: Fireside, 1988), 206.

4   Jerome Shapiro, *Atomic Bomb Cinema: The Apocalyptic Imagination on Film* (New York and London: Routledge, 2002), 179.

5   Shapiro, *Atomic Bomb Cinema: The Apocalyptic Imagination on Film*, 177.

6   Danny Peary, *Cult Movies 3* (New York: Fireside, 1988), 33.

7   Keith M. Booker, *Alternate Americas: Science Fiction Film and American Culture* (Westport: Praeger Publications, 2006), 178-184.

8   Paul M Sammon, *Future Noir: The Making of Blade Runner* (New York: HarperPaperbacks, 1996), 18-19.

9   Ian Scott, *American Politics in Hollywood Film* (Edinburgh: Edinburgh University Press, 2000), 109.

10   Christopher Palmer, *Philip K. Dick: Exhilaration and Terror of the Postmodern* (Liverpool: Liverpool University Press, 2003), 9.

11   Chris Rodley, *Lynch on Lynch* (London: Faber and Faber, 1997, 2005), 134.

12   Rodley, *Lynch on Lynch*, 136.

13   Rodley, *Lynch on Lynch*, 136.

14   Charles Drazin, *Blue Velvet: A Bloomsbury Movie Guide* (New York: Blooms-bury Publications, 1998), 40.

Chapter Eight
Films from the 1990s

After twelve years of staunch Republican leadership in the nation's presidency, the decade underwent a formidable character shift with the arrival of Bill Clinton and his renovated vision of the Democratic Party. The combination of the egalitarian Clinton White House and our country's strengthening economy redressed the cultural disengagement of a large generation of young professionals looking for material success and social responsibility. Although the administration of George H.W. Bush had rallied the nation in the first Gulf War (1991), the senior GOP leadership lost its bearing, and independent candidate Ross Perot maneuvered the voting public with populist themes at Bush's expense. Despite Perot opening opportunities to new ideas in the political horizon, his ability to hurt or influence Clinton was insubstantial as the decade unfolded. Sexual and racial politics dominated Bush's controversial nomination of Clarence Thomas to the Supreme Court in 1991. Anita Hill found herself a reluctant martyr to women's rights as a result, and the nation heard more graphic testimony than necessary. The country had accepted the HIV scourge, knowing that medical innovations supported the longevity and the quality of life for AIDS patients. Hillary Clinton failed to deliver a progressive and ambitious national health program; Bill Clinton learned in his first presidential week that it was sheer folly to take on the military brass. Inspired by Harry Truman, Clinton attempted to liberalize the armed forces by decriminalizing homosexuality, but the political compromise ended up as a bald slogan and a monstrous hypocrisy—"Don't Ask, Don't Tell." The corporate world celebrated an unparalleled number of mergers and company repositioning. The unsettling rise of militias and anti-government cults generated a genuine concern about civilian safety. The 1995 Oklahoma City bombing by Timothy McVeigh, killing 168 Americans devastated the nation. That same year, O.J. Simpson's murder trial perplexed American society and polarized blacks from whites, particularly following the 1992 Los Angeles riots and the acquittal of the Los Angeles police beating of Rodney King. At the end of the decade, the horrific Columbine High School massacre pierced the nation's conscience and society's justification for private gun ownership. In the last years of the decade, the exponential power of home computers and the ease of Internet travel transformed the country and the balance of the world. International boundaries vanished and governmental control was weakened due to electronic retail commerce. The Y2K scare in 1999 had elements of farce and *Dr. Strangelove*-esque disturbance; our faith in computers temporarily evaporated. Equally farcical, the 1998 media frenzy over Bill Clinton's dalliance with intern Monica Lewinsky disabled the proper mechanics of daily government in Washington. *The X-Files* (1993-2002) secured a sizable television cult following and rap music moved rapidly into the cultural idiom. Hollywood actors turned directors—Clint Eastwood, Mel Gibson, and Kevin Costner—mastered personal expression and scored Academy Awards for *Unforgiven* (1992), *Braveheart* (1995), and *Dances with Wolves* (1990) respectively. Steven Spielberg surprised filmgoers with his somber, mature holocaust work, *Schindler's List* (1993). In the world of theatre, political playwright Tony Kushner won the 1991 Pulitzer Prize for *Angels in America*—a work highly focused on AIDS and intolerance that stretched the parameters of Broadway fare. *Harry Potter* books revolutionized children's reading habits. Contributing to the national literature were William Gaddis, Daniel Goldhagen, Frank McCourt, Toni Morrison, E. Annie Proulx, Philip Roth, and Susan Sontag. Causing a spectacular sensation in professional golf and a new access to the sport was the debut of Tiger Woods in 1996. Finally, introducing a change in the ways that studios market films was cultish *The Blair Witch Project* (1999)—a low cost docudrama horror story that built an impressive following on the Internet.

Delicatessen (1991)

For a change of venue and delicacy, a French cult film by two directors exploiting the taboo of cannibalism revived silent film comedy gags with the dangerous counterforce posed by underground vegetarian terrorists. This offbeat black satire from Jean-Pierre Jeunet and Marc Caro presents a depressed and despoiled society that stands after apocalyptic circumstances but remains retrofitted to the 1950s in post-war Europe and remnants of the French Vichy period (with all the material and moral compromising of that era).[1] We see an 'end of the world' variation on the expansive desert cruelty of George Miller's *Road Warrior* (1981) and the totalitarian madness within Terry Gilliam's *Brazil* (1985). Additionally, Jeunet and Caro incorporate a broad swatch of cannibal myth and fiction of Sweeney Todd, the mythic demon barber of Fleet Street.

Louison (Dominique Pinon), the laconic, clowning hero of *Delicatessen*, is an employed circus attraction. His semi-sweet screen persona harkens back to the great silent comedians Charlie Chaplin and Buster Keaton. In the few days he has taken occupancy as the custodian within the dilapidated dwelling owned and operated by a malevolent butcher Clapet, Louison has developed a romantic tie with the butcher's mousy, bespectacled daughter Julie. Julie plays the cello and Louison plays the musical carpenter's saw; when they eventually play a sonata together it is as good as sexual consummation. Falling in love is not unique for the young damsel, since she swoons for each "superintendent de jour." Unifying the story are two little boys and their special youthful point of view, who watch the farfetched activities within the housing complex. In 1956, Claude de Autuant-Lara's macabre comic predecessor to *Delicatessen, La Traversée de Paris* (Crossing Paris) also featured a perfidious butcher, a black market, and wartime occupation rationing.[2] Jeunet and Caro have not reinvented that earlier film so much as updated the sensibility of French butchery and callousness.

The outrageous tenants create a memorable mural of insane, urban life. The residents are mindful to pay their rent on time or they will vanish to feed the carnivores. Madam Interligator hears threatening voices in her head urging her on to construct elaborate Rube Goldberg suicide machines, while her husband spends time recycling bicycle patches to prolong the life of a condom. Her deaf mother, with tin cans attached to her feet, knits her way into eternity. The Kube brothers make small canisters that reproduce the sounds of contented cows. Upstairs, in a flood of water, is a legion of frogs and snails under the supervision of Frog Man. A prostitute and assorted gangsters fill out the decadent roster.

Julie, fearing that Louison will leave in the manner of his predecessors, searches the sewers to alert the armed resistance fighters, the rubber-clad Troglodists. She will provide them her father's bounty in exchange for Louison's safety. Given Clapet's immediate resentment towards the young lover, Louison's survival is the main action of the film.

Beginning in 1980, Jeuenet and Caro have collaborated for over fifteen years, making short films, television commercials, and music videos, graduating into two feature films. *The City of Lost Children* (La Cité des Enfants Perdus) came out four years after *Delicatessen* and continued their signature style of kinetically visual vignettes, kaleidoscopic effects, and grotesque incongruities that resemble hallucinogenic Brothers Grimm fairy tales. Marc Caro brought to the collaboration his fecund flair as an artist and comic book creator, while Jean-Pierre Jeunet emphasized his finesse with actors and dramatic context. Their first project together, 1981's *Le Bunker de la Dernière Rafale* (The Last Blast Bunker), punctuated the virulent paranoia soldiers confront underground. *The Last Blast* had forecasted more wartime obsession in the most recent solo directing by Jeunet in 2004, *A Very Long Engagement* (Un Long Dimanche de Fiançailles).

Landlord Clapet's baroque edifice is a living hell, the embodiment of a diseased carcass twisted with varicose piping that carries the private discussions of others. The public staircase forms the spine while the downstairs deli outlines the face and mouth of this metaphoric dying entity. The essential garbage chute serves as the building's rectum. The two children on the stairway foyer represent a shred of innocence among the corruption, and the filmmakers do much to stress the spiritual affinities between Louison and these young boys. Clearly, the innocence preserved is not marred because the children smoke cigarettes and sense when couples are copulating behind closed doors.

Delicatessen is a landmark film for tricking the eye and ear on the nature of beauty and squalor. Many of the interior sets are lovingly embellished in thrift store regalia, outrageous clutter, and monochromatic richness in sepia tones or ugly orange hues. Innovative cinematographer Darius Khondji used a resilvering process to maximize the dimly lit, painterly aspects of the compositions.[3] The absurdist humor is often forced by Jeunet and Caro, but there is evidence of affection for what is unmistakably neurotic portraiture. The filmmakers are known for fastidious, painstaking film production and holding at bay the cannibalistic press before completing their story. In spirit and sensibility, Jeunet and Caro seem to be artistic cousins of the highly visual fabulists Terry Gilliam and

Tim Burton. Less is not more; more is better. *Delicatessen* indulges in very tight close-ups and wide-angle shots rendering attractive and hideous faces into topographic maps. Jeunet and Caro's inventive camera work highlight odd angles, ludicrous tracking shots, aggressive editing, and live actor animation.

Their last feature together, *The City of Lost Children* (La Cité des Enfants Perdus), picked up on the peripheral two boys in *Delicatessen* and invested far more of the filmmakers' fascination for orphaned children in a land of decay. Replacing the taboo of murder and cannibalism with the illicit themes of kidnapping and human cloning, *The City of Lost Children* is somewhat less disturbing but far more confusing. Perhaps it is the added layer of fake Jules Verne-like inventions that reduces the needed emotional accessibility to the filmmakers' second project. Crossing over the Atlantic to Hollywood and to science fiction horror, Jeunet went on to direct *Alien—Resurrection* (1997) with art direction from Caro.[4] Jeunet's light-hearted romantic comedy *Amélie* (2001) brought him vast international attention, major honors in France and in Europe, and several Academy Award nominations.

Delicatessen was originally called *La Concierge est dans L'escalier* (The Concierge is in the Stairs) and the title change lent ironic possibilities for marketing. A favorite montage sequence in the film became the American trailer. Louison, using his trouser suspenders for aerial leverage, paints the ceiling while the tenants assemble toys, knit, and play the cello, and Clapet fornicates with his mistress on a squeaky bedspring mattress. The bedspring sets the tempo for the building's occupants until the butcher sexually climaxes and each corollary action follows suit. The film's detached irony guides us comfortably through the muck and pain.

In the film canon of cult, the gruesome theme of consuming human flesh runs the gamut from Paul Bartel's black comedy *Eating Raoul* (1982) to the widely banned, horrific pseudo-documentary *Cannibal Holocaust* (1980) by Ruggero Deodato. Although *Delicatessen* demonstrates consistent visceral and intellectual animus toward European and American fleshy consumerism, the film steers clear of Deodato's violently pornographic approach to all things corporal. While *Eating Raoul* emphasizes American kitsch, sketch comedy, and improvisational forethought, *Delicatessen* is painterly, meticulous, and often artistically vain. The many marvelous aesthetic conceits within *Delicatessen* support the film's artists and artistry sometimes at the expense of the story content. One need not fault Jeunet and Caro for these decisions and for their playfulness, since they succeeded in composing an illustrated tone poem on, perchance, the last tenement on earth.

Naked Lunch (1991)

Canadian director David Cronenberg has been proclaimed as a disturbing film artist who obsesses over the mutation and mutilation of the human body and the corollary trauma to the human personality, particularly in the first twenty years of his output. Comfortably, Cronenberg had positioned himself in the eyes of critics as a master of nuanced horror and neurotic science fiction. In more recent years he has moved into psychological mystery and menace, relying less on physiological themes and graphic shock. After completing his early masterpiece, *Dead Ringer,* in 1988, Cronenberg adjusted his philosophic directives about the nature of guilt, sin, and madness.

The ostensible basis for *Dead Ringers* comes from a morbid historical account of biological twins, Drs. Cyril and Stewart Marcus, found decomposed and semi-nude in their disheveled Manhattan apartment in 1975. With *Naked Lunch*, Cronenberg was intrigued by the possibility to embroider real life analogues from author William S. Burroughs's controversial novel from 1962. In the span of three years, the combination of *Dead Ringers* and *Naked Lunch* created new opportunities for Cronenberg, in view of his growing international prestige as an auteur still obsessed with the human body.

"One of our touchstones for reality is our bodies," Cronenberg had explained, "And yet they too are by definition ephemeral. So to whatever degree we center our reality—and on understanding reality—in our bodies, we are surrendering that sense of reality to our bodies' emperality."[5]

Veering away from the anthology element of Burroughs' book, Cronenberg centers a story on William Lee (a man loosely inspired by Burroughs), who has contentions with his wife Joan. By profession a New York City pest exterminator, William is cognizant of Joan's open infidelity with his friends and her appropriating his expensive insect chemicals for self-medicating recreation. Perhaps this is not the most fascinating plotting device for a feature narrative, but both the filmed *Naked Lunch* and the book have little to do with American realism, literary logic, and psychological profiles. Yet *Naked Lunch* misbehaves too as a piece of symbolic substance. Characters representing novelist Jack Kerouac and poet Allen Ginsberg betray Joan's habit to Bill. Becoming more detached, Bill is taken in by the police and he wrestles hard to find a grip with reality. His overriding fear is that he has succumbed to hallucinations brought on by the potent insect powder. In this picture, the bugs start out small and grow exponentially. This downward spiral for Bill leads him to think Joan is a secret agent under the control of a giant insect. Bill gets the news from the bug and the bug's order to Bill is reprehensible: murder his wife and make it real tasty.

The syllogism is played out wryly. Bill and Joan bizarrely enact their "William Tell" routine in keeping with the parallel to Burroughs' espousal tragedy one miserable night in Mexico City. Bill's gun misses the target atop Joan's head and the bullet pierces her. Needing to flee the city, Bill flies off to Interzone—a metaphysical region well established in Burroughs' novel and evoking Morocco's most solicitous city for illicit pleasures, Tangier. To explore the unchartered life in the Interzone, Bill endures a lot of pain in pursuit of an artistic goal. Cronenberg expresses the anguish of writing and living in abject exile. In Kafkaesque fashion, the articulate bug is both muse and machine for Bill. As tendered by actor Peter Weller, Bill is stoic and taciturn. It is difficult to read his emotional apparatus compared to the relative transparency of the twin brothers in *Dead Ringers*. To ensure that Bill can be no more isolated in this existential state, Cronenberg introduces a man-sized insect, Mugwump, and a humungous Brazilian centipede. Complicating the incoherent interactions is a deranged doctor, Bentway, a colleague writer, and a rascal playboy.

What may not be clear to the film audience is the story's reliance on unforgiving drugs, on Burroughs' troubled life, and the inner sanctum of Cronenberg's poetic analysand.[6] Bill's crisis may strike many as a pretentious one so ostentatious are the high minded and elite cultural references in the film. It would seem that Cronenberg is less concerned with the cognitive life of the narrative fable since Burroughs' book defies coherent plotting. With repeated viewing, *Naked Lunch* intensifies with comic possibilities enhanced by the steady deadpan of actor Peter Weller. The film's supporting, intellectual cast is absurdly impeccable and perfectly wry: Judy Davis, Ian Holm, Roy Schneider, and Julian Sands. While Peter Weller cannot approximate the haunting injuries and private transgressions in Jeremy Iron's superior work in *Dead Ringers*, Weller manages to capture much of William Burroughs' flat ironies, personality defects, and unapologetic moral indifference to an unsentimental soul.

Naked Lunch could be more satirical, accessible, and darkly pleasurable; and yet, for some viewers, the vile talking bugs might be as good as surrealistic comedy ever gets. Still, Cronenberg avoids any approach toward popular entertainment given that his neurotic obsessions and their underlying cultural taboos resist safe appropriation or commercialization. Cronenberg's achievement here is the fusion of art design and the production of cinematic monstrosity.[7] Many will recognize the insect's talking orifice as a mammal's anus. An aloof esthete would probably draw closer to *Naked Lunch* over Cronenberg's *The Fly* (1986), despite their shared pessimism and the prominence of large insects in both films. Importantly, there is a genuine, cathartic charge for a cerebral misanthrope on Burroughs' journey. After all, some articulate madness can be reassuring and this fictionalized Morocco has certain advantages over more traditional vacations. The elements of irrationality are shown in a casual, accidental manner to support Cronenberg's deliberate perversions.

The confident cinematography by Peter Suschitzky, who began teaming up with Cronenberg in *Dead Ringers*, is superlative with studious, interior compositions and countless exotic details, keeping tempers claustrophobic and unnerving. Less successful is the cavalcade of well-lit, repulsive bug puppetry. The beat jazz horns, that carry much of Howard Shore's musical score, work splendidly with the film's opening credits, and on occasion enrich the best segments of *Naked Lunch*. Acid trips were a commodity in the 1960s, which makes the psilocybin dementia of *Naked Lunch's* 1950s all the more perplexing to literalists. Cooking bug powder in a teaspoon for injection suggests heroin's deadening invitation and not a wild escapade into Kafka's fecund imagination.

In Canada, Cronenberg had magically morphed from a national embarrassment (purveyor of shock horror) into the nation's great film director.[8] Cronenberg moved on to two other exceptional, critically acknowledged films that did not stray from topics of lasting discomfort, *Crash* (1996)—about accident motor victims who bond sexually, and *The History of Violence* (2005)—a morality tale about an American hero's gangland heritage. What might be indicative about the

future work of Cronenberg is the recent absence of unreal grotesquery and tera-
tologic fears found in *Rabid* (1977), *The Brood* (1979), *Scanners* (1981), *Videodrome* (1983), and *eXistenZ* (1999). All of Cronenberg's films teeter on the edge
of inhumanity, and for Cronenberg's detractors; the inhumanity contaminates
any chance for balance and optimism. The cult audience in support of *Naked
Lunch* and the rest of the Cronenberg *oeuvre* either gleans the artist's visceral
originality or the painful shock of Cronenberg's confessionals.

Run Lola Run/ Lola Rennt (1998)

The English version title of Tom Tykwer's film sounds like a primer for kinder-
garten. Yes, Lola has brilliant red hair cut just an inch beyond a spiky bob.
When she sprints, her mane seems to catch fire. Her boyfriend, Manni, acknowl-
edges her beauty, but he has vainly compromised his relationship thanks to his
runaway smuggling enterprise. What appears to be Manni's last hurrah endan-
gers Manni and Lola. She has to deliver Manni and his stash of 100,000
Deutsche Marks to a meeting with his crime boss, Ronnie. However, her moped
was swiped. Impatient, her boyfriend turns to the subway and inadvertently
forgets the money on the train—distracted by train inspectors expecting fare
tickets. A destitute man picks up the bag of cash. Manni phones Lola and declares that he will be dead unless he can reclaim in the money for Ronnie. She
promises to find the sum of money in time. Still, Manni's desperation leads him
to hold up a nearby supermarket. In a variation of quantum mechanics theory,
German filmmaker Tykwer provides alternative conclusions in triple parallel
universes to this expository set-up. The hyper-pulsed, twenty minute sequence
of Lola's desperate marathon with minor differences greatly impacts the outcome of the tale.

   Run Lola Run became an instant crowd pleaser in its debut at top film festivals such as Venice, Montreal, Toronto, Sundance, and the Film Society of
Lincoln Center in New York. Immediate to supportive critics were Tykwer's
verve, wit, and subversion on some news thread more suitable for tabloid clip-
ping. Lola's audience is not asked to judge her moral actions but rather to race
along with her on a dubious goal. Moreover, the film symbolized a clean break
with German cinema's self-reflection and repressed history, heralding a new
voice in the post-Fassbinder generation.[9] *Run Lola Run* is a boldly creative if not
belabored exercise on style first; the notion that fate is an unfixed proposition
serves as forceful motivation for the film's justification. Of course, the film
exists as a reverberation on media since the cartoon image of Lola running lands
on a television screen during a dramatic sequence.

   The journey to Lola's lover should not end happily but the phenomenon of
repetition supplants the concern of mortal consequence and the imagery of spi-
raling (e.g., winding stairs, roulette wheel, woman's hair bun) infuses many
ordinary moments of the film.[10] These revolutions of Lola's reality has a shading
of life guided by supernatural prescience. In the first rendition of this triptych,

Lola speeds to her father's bank but he denies her. Her father wounds her further by declaring that he is not her father. Passing an ambulance, she hurries to Manni but arrives too late. The burglary is taking place and she impulsively aids his crime. Lola is swept up by a power greater than romance. Fleeing the store, Manni and Lola are engulfed by the police. A cop shoots Lola.

In the second rendition which approximates the moment of Lola's death, the action jumps back to the initial phone call from Manni. Leaving her apartment, Lola is stalled by a child on the stairway. She gets to the bank somewhat later than in the first rendition and as a consequence Lola has a sharp exchange with her father's mistress. All this leads to Lola robbing the bank and getting the cash to her lover. Trying to catch a ride on the ambulance, Lola causes the vehicle to smash into workers carrying a window pane. Ironically, Lola gets to Manni just as he is hit fatally by the ambulance. As in the first rendition, a free association sequence plays out with the lovers in bed, proclaiming genuine love for one another.

The third rendition, Lola seems to have learned things in a precognitive arrangement. Like Bill Murray's character in *Groundhog Day* (1993), Lola has improved her ability to complete a task aided by the precise replay of the scene. Further, she moves more quickly, flying over stairs where she once slipped, and prevents a motor accident involving her father's colleague. The chain reaction herein has the colleague chauffeuring Lola's father to work and preempting Lola from catching him at the bank. She enters a casino and plays roulette. Miraculously Lola wins two rounds and 127,000 Deutsche Marks. The money in hand, she must beat the clock. Employing the same ambulance as before, Lola hopes to reach Manni. The vehicle is transporting a bank security guard. Lola knows the guard and places his hand in hers. Her response to the injured man is very telling in light of the greater crisis with Manni. Switching focus to Manni, he discovers the subway vagrant on a bicycle with the 100,000 Deutsche Marks. Forgiving these coincidences, Manni recovers the loot and gets it to Ronnie in time. The final moments of this version have Lola greeting Manni while he inquires what's in her bag. Certainly, a more idealized ending could not be wished.

Franka Potente portrays Lola quite knowingly, and she gives Lola, frame by frame, accessibility to the camera's addictiveness. Potente renders her character as an action figure for a music video while at the same time secures her character's independence from the prison of posturing. She interprets Lola as an attractive free agent and as a heroine who does not necessarily endorse Manni's lifestyle. Because of the brevity of each reality rendition, Potente commands sufficient vitality and existential purpose. It would be another matter altogether to maintain Lola's iconoclastic identity if Tykwer's film were a linear arc for eighty minutes. In additional, Lola has a realization as she empowers her lone female body contraposed to an oppressive cityscape. Her femininity is a radical departure from her mother's identity.[11] Evidently, Tykwer was not making a softer version of *Bonnie and Clyde* (1967) nor was he transforming his dramatic characters into a hip, animated shock-fest as typified by Robert Rodriguez's *Sin City* (2005). To some critics, including Janet Maslin of *The New York Times*, the

Tykwer had fashioned an engaging, interactive video game for cineastes.[12] Critical to the director's sensibility, the soundtrack percolates with techno-music to carry the minimal text. Contrasting the kinetic overlay, Tykwer also applied instrumental chords reflecting Charles Ives's *The Unanswered Question* and an upbeat ballad sung by Dinah Washington, "What a Difference a Day Made".

Run Lola Run was a career turning point for Tykwer, who was thirty-four at the time of the film's release. He went on to direct *The Princess and the Warrior* (Der Krieger und die Kaiserin) (2000), *Heaven* (2002), and *Perfume: The Story of a Murderer* (Das Parfum:Die Geschichte eines Mörders) (2006), but his fleeting moments with lovely charismatic Lola have outdistanced everything in his canon to date.

Notes:

1   Anne L. Bower, ed., *Reel Food: Essays on Film and Food*; Kyri Watson Claflin, *Jean-Pierre Jeunet and Marc Caro's Delicatessen* (New York and Abingdon: Routledge, 2004), 237-238.

2   Bower, ed., *Reel Food: Essays on Film and Food*; Claflin, *Jean-Pierre Jeunet and Marc Caro's Delicatessen*, 240.

3   Richard Dyer, *Se7en (BFI Modern Classics)* (London: British Film Institute, 1999), 61.

4   David Thomson, *The Alien Quartet: A Bloomsbury Movie Guide* (New York and London: Bloomsbury Publications, 1998), 136.

5   Chris Rodley, *Cronenberg on Cronenberg* (London: Faber and Faber, 1992), 145.

6   Carl Royer and Diana Royer, *The Spectacle of Isolation in Horror Films: Dark Parades* (Binghamton: Haworth Press 2005), 68.

7   William Beard, *The Artist as Monster: The Cinema of David Cronenberg* (Toronto: University of Toronto Press, 2006), 103.

8   Beard, *The Artist as Monster: The Cinema of David Cronenberg*, 287.

9   Maurice Yacowar, *Run Lola Run: Renn for your Life,* An Article from Queen's Quarterly Vol. 106, Issue 4 (December 1999), 556-65.

10   Craig Detweiler and Barry Taylor, *A Matrix of Meaning: Finding God in Pop Culture* (Grand Rapids: Baker Academic, 2003), 179.

11   Agnes C. Muller, ed., *German Pop Culture: How "American" Is It?* Barbara Kosta, *Tom Tykwer's Run Lola Run and The Usual Suspects* (Ann Arbor, University of Michigan Press, 2004), 170.

12   Janet Maslin, *Film Festival Review; A Dangerous Game With Several Endings* (review of *Run Lola Run*), *The New York Times* (March 26, 1999).

Chapter Nine
Films from the 2000s

This most recent decade exudes an air of elusiveness and uncertainty. Astronomers demoted Pluto and cast this small heavenly body out of the elite society of planets. The last *Harry Potter* book was published in 2007, yet the Hollywood franchising of young Harry speeds ahead like an unstoppable juggernaut. At the same time, it took the long running hit animation show *The Simpsons* (1989—) eighteen years to jump from television to feature film. Al Gore won the nation's popular vote in 2000, and never moved into the White House. Instead, he earned a film Oscar and alerted us to global warming. George W. Bush became a two-term president, outdistancing his father and startling many analysts who underestimated his ability to win elections. Surprising many was the affectionate alliance between Bill Clinton and George Herbert Walker Bush in their altruistic travels. Certainly, the most traumatizing event was the heinous September 11th attack by Al-Qaeda on American soil. The catastrophe unleashed legislation and security measures that have compromised, in the eyes of many historians, American democracy and our Bill of Rights. Osama bin Laden is still at large, but the nation has become embroiled in a war without end in Iraq. The tragedy that befell New Orleans and its environs in the wake of Hurricane Katrina caused tremendous economic and political shock waves but for the nation, and chipped away at the White House's political capital. Of significance on another front was the fear of gay marriage and its formidable impact on the 2004 election. In ironic counterpoint—the 2005 Academy Award for best direction went to Ang Lee for, *Brokeback Mountain*—a discreet story about homosexual cowboys.

Breaking barriers, Oscars for best acting were awarded to several African Americans—Denzel Washington, Halle Berry, Jamie Foxx, Morgan Freeman, Forest Whittaker, and Jennifer Hudson. Shock radio jock Howard Stern left his FM woes at the FCC's doorstep and found greater freedom on satellite broadcasting, while racially insensitive Don Imus was fired by CBS Radio for taunting female basketball players at Rutgers. The national passion for baseball statistics, skewered in the late 1990s by the steroid scandals, reached climax when Barry Bonds shattered Hank Aaron's lifetime 755 home run record. Jon Stewart and Stephen Colbert brought new cachet to fake news broadcasts on cable. Noted literature of the period was penned by Jonathan Franzen, Alice Sebold, Cormac McCarthy, Suzan-Lori Parks, and Michael Chabon. In the financial arena, popular high-tech and Internet stocks were reappraised after the technology bubble burst in March 2000. Nevertheless, the public fascination for rapid investment gratification did not completely fade away. Real estate baron Donald Trump entered reality television with his hit show *The Apprentice*. World media mogul Rupert Murdoch was triumphant in purchasing the *Wall Street Journal* in 2007, signally a new chapter in American business journalism. The high school and college demographic helped propel social networking in cyberspace with Facebook and MySpace while YouTube engendered a video immediacy of unlimited dimension, media savvy, and consequence. Indeed, the Democratic presidential candidates debating in 2007 demonstrated that, in some essential regard, YouTube enjoyed equal footing with cable giant CNN. Unusual in the 2008 presidential campaign was the prominence of two Democratic Party frontrunners, Hilary Clinton and Barack Obama, suggesting a new era of opportunity in casting beyond the traditional mix of white male candidates.

Hedwig and the Angry Inch (2001)

The Rocky Horror Picture Show (1975) may be arguably the most identified cult film in popular parlance. For thirty years, the legion of fans who attend late night screenings dressed as members of the cast, versed in every line of dialogue, and rehearsed to sing and dance every musical number help demonstrate the staying power and fanaticism of *Rocky Horror* fever. So it comes as no surprise to discover the androgynous DNA of this quintessential cult movie in John Cameron Mitchell's *Hedwig and the Angry Inch*. Like *The Rocky Horror Picture Show*, Mitchell's production began as live musical theatre before morphing into film; common to *Rocky Horror* and *Hedwig* is the reliance on a charismatic drag queen at the center of the event and the blurring of sexual personalities. Mitchell's production nearly anticipates the full frontal transsexual nudity of *Transamerica* (2005) *Hedwig* is analyzed bluntly but with admiration by *The Village Voice* which called it a rock musical about castration. More importantly, the review highlights that Hansel/Hedwig never claims to want become a woman in order to become an American. Amy Taubin, reviewing for *The Village Voice*, also laments that the last shot could not do what *Transamerica* did effortlessly.[1]

Mitchell's concept draws on his life as the son of an army general who was posted in Germany before the fall of the Berlin Wall. The Berlin setting is an inspired component of *Hedwig*'s mystique as a rock film and as a portrait of Euro-trash. The remarkable identity of Hedwig was based loosely on a risqué German who once served as a nanny for the Mitchell clan. The creative musical lodestone in *Hedwig* was part and parcel of the androgynous 1970s glam-rock explosion that brought early fame to David Bowie, Iggy Pop, and other bisexual or androgynous pop stars. In addition, Mitchell was making full use of political performance art to heighten the theatricality of the concert narrative.

After workshop performances for mostly gay audiences in small New York clubs, the stage version of *Hedwig* opened to adoring reviews in February 1998, Off Broadway at the Jane Street Theatre on the fringe of the meatpacking district. Mitchell, starring as the title character, connected powerfully to his young, downtown audiences as he confessed in song the very depths of his sexual pain and misanthropic travails. Nearly fifty years after Ed Wood's *Glen or Glenda*, we meet another marginal misfit in cosmic freefall. Mitchell's Hedwig is a casualty of inept sex change surgery, and Hedwig goes on tour to tell the world. Certainly, Hedwig is searching for the perfect soul mate to complete her teleology. As the show is conceived, it is Hedwig's unfortunate lot to end up loveless and performing in the least prestigious lounges in America.

Mitchell commits passionately to a back story about Hedwig as Hansel, a gay German youth, who meets and loves an American army officer, Luther. Hansel proposes that he joins the master sergeant back in the United States. Luther counters with the promise of a gender change operation for Hansel, thus allowing for a marriage certificate and visa out of Germany. Or, to put it bluntly, Hansel's lover states, "To walk away, you gotta leave something behind."[2] Hansel's mother gives him her passport (designated for Hedwig) and selects a mediocre physician for the procedure. Tragically, the surgery leaves Hansel with a one inch stub and a terrible vertical scar. Hansel becomes Hedwig and goes as Luther's bride to Junction City, Kansas. On their first anniversary, Hedwig is dumped inside a low-life trailer park—oddly timed with the fall of the Berlin Wall. She is left to whore herself within the local military base. But her better nature lifts Hedwig to build an ambitious rock band comprised of Korean wives, and Hedwig become the group's fabulous, sardonic lead singer.

Soon after, Hedwig meets teen Tommy Speck, a quiet, unassuming soul. They cultivate a tight connection and Hedwig creates a few songs for Tommy. This interlude ends up haunting Hedwig when Tommy, with the use of Hedwig's compositions, becomes a rock superstar. Hedwig cannot reconcile the inequity of Tommy's mega-theatre venues in contrast to the dives she plays. Once more, destiny has been excessively cruel to Hedwig/Hansel. Adding to Hedwig's anguish is her lost youth and the farce of living in an adopted land.

Stephen Trask wrote the impressive music and lyrics for *Hedwig*. Key numbers such as "Wig in the Box" and "Wicked Little Town" carry heft and punch. Trask achieves a kaleidoscope effect modulating edgy punk rock songs with country western "Sugar Daddy" and coffeehouse "The Origin of Love." The musical incongruities work as well as the basic cultural concept behind *Hedwig*.[3] Accepting the incongruity of Marlene Dietrich in the cowboy film *Destry Rides Again* (1939) is as plausible as Hedwig in Kansas. The *Hedwig* stage version and the *Hedwig* film have divergent endings. The play expresses fusion between Hedwig and Tommy—either as an adumbration of a single identity or to complete the song "The Origin of Love," illuminating the myth in Plato's Symposium about the physical division of two-headed, eight-limbed entities. The movie ends showing Hedwig and Tommy in a car crash leading to Hedwig's stream of consciousness. The parade of dreamlike images and scenes filtering through Hedwig's mind involve Hedwig's sudden world fame, slumming through backwater lounges, and a farewell scene with Tommy inside a dark cavernous concert hall, and a packed concert where Hedwig celebrates with the song "Midnight Radio." Finally, Hedwig sees herself without clothes in a dank alley. Her tattoo depicting two half moon faces transforms into a single countenance. Hedwig leaves the alley and disappears from the screen.

Mitchell, in plain clothes and out of character, has a convincing physical re-semblance to comic Dana Carvey, and similar to Carvey's sweet demeanor, Mitchell's persona is polar opposite to Hedwig's. Mitchell, clearly fatigued, left the role during the long New York stage run. Realizing the film version gave Mitchell new celebrity worldwide and preserved the outstanding performance he displayed on stage; yet the film also distanced significantly the spontaneity and cabaret electricity of the live *Hedwig* show. Moreover, the film provided many literal enactments that were narrated more powerfully and self-dramatized by Mitchell on stage. Many critics and fans of *Hedwig* debate the sexual politics of the story. Is Hedwig principally a drag artist, a transvestite, or a transsexual? Is the character using femininity to disguise devolving aspects of masculinity, adding to modern feminist theory—Michele Montrelay's idea of masquerade?[4] Would director Ed Wood add a new segment in his *Glen or Glenda* to accom-modate Hedwig's dilemma? If Hedwig represents a freak show candidacy first and foremost, is she counterproductive to affirmative elements in queer theory and critical gender analysis? An interesting side note: Ally Sheedy took on the role as the first actress to play Hedwig on stage in 1999 but she had great diffi-culty winning the critics and the fans. Perhaps the gender confusion went one degree too far with Sheedy's femininity based in reality and the necessary con-cept of homo-duality.[5]

Purists who love *Hedwig* on stage mention that the one-person show mysti-que, carried by the anonymous backup band, is mostly lost on screen. The anec-dotal feel and bawdiness of the stage actor's banter are missed often in the lavish movie, since Mitchell chose not to produce a self-documentary *Hedwig*. Other liberties were taken by Mitchell. A major background player in the film version is the punningly named Phyllis Stein, Hedwig's agent and manager. On screen Stein (Andrea Martin) is a nurturing support to Hedwig, whereas on stage she is alluded to as diffident and uncaring. Nonetheless, *Hedwig and the Angry Inch* took the 2001 Sundance Audience Award and honored Mitchell for best direc-tion. And in the proud tradition of *The Rocky Horror Picture Show*, *Hedwig* is heavily merchandized through websites and stores; Mitchell's film can be seen best in late night showings around the nation in countless cities and states. Even Hedwig's tattoo is very much in demand today.

The Ring (2002)

Within Gore Verbinski's big grossing film is perhaps the ultimate home viewing cult experience. As most young people know, seeing this short video condemns the viewer to a death sentence. The conceit of this urban legend about a video-tape curse helps fuel *The Ring*, but it is the least appealing component that makes the movie's experience so accomplished and sparked remakes and se-quels. Someone knows someone who had a tragic accident—and you must heed the advisory warning at all costs. Forewarned, the curse might be avoided (one can see the accursed video anytime on YouTube, avoiding the Blockbuster DVD rental fee and any late penalties).

Verbinski brings a new twist to the cliché about ghosts in the machine. Re-imagined for an American teenage market, *The Ring* takes the basic details of Hideo Nakata's 1998 Japanese film *Ringu* and upholsters a more opulent super-natural horror, including a riveting scene of galloping horses on a ferry. None-theless, the 2002 production uses digital effects sparingly to emphasize the dra-matic blurring between reality and technical media.[6] The two film versions come from Koji Suzuki's novel, *Ring*. In the American rendition, a Seattle reporter named Rachel (played by Naomi Watts) is compelled by her sister to research the death of Rachel's niece. What makes Rachel's character striking is that she's a poor candidate for mother of the year; she's work obsessed; she's estranged from her son's father. The tortuous transformation Rachel makes in the course of this story rehabilitates her and her primal maternal instinct. In her opening scene with her son Aidan at school, Rachel appears finely tuned as a beautiful blonde narcissist who is always late picking up her son. The teacher notes Ra-chel's disregard. Established early are Aidan's psychic talents and sickly child's vulnerabilities. Aidan has been sketching revolting images of cadavers. Later that evening, he tells his mother, "We don't have enough time." The implication of his statement concerns the impending videotape threat.

Prior to meeting Rachel and Aidan, the film's prologue showcases two teen-agers in a heated discussion about an eerie mountain cabin visit a week ago. Katie admits to her friend Becca to looking at a pirate video at the cabin. Becca informs Katie that anyone who dares to watch this video gets an anonymous phone call with a two word message, "seven days." One week after experiencing the tape, the viewer perishes from fright. Distinguish from what Becca and Katie discuss to what then transpired. What proceeds is a devastating psychic attack inside the house, with televisions hyper-animated, and Katie is shocked into annihilation. Becca enters a mental hospital.

That evening Rachel, Katie's aunt, traces Katie's steps to a remote motel cabin. The clerk gives her the untitled video cassette. It is Rachel's misfortune to have then watched the video tape and to have made a copy to take back with her to assist her investigation. Let us assume that the curse would also work on burned DVD copies and TiVo for those wondering about the obsolescence of VHS tape. The copy in Rachel's possession is for Aidan's father to study since he's technically proficient with electronic media production. After her hospital visit to Becca, Rachel is vaguely aware that a phone rings after one views the tape, signaling days remains before a hideous death.

At this segment in the Verbinski film, Rachel concerns herself with the mysterious tape for forensic clues. The grainy black and white images features: a suffering animal, maggots, bleak reflection in a mirror of a haunted woman, visual static, a ladder to nowhere, the moon, an endless well, and a fly crawling over a television screen. Careful investigation steers Rachel to identifying Anna Morgan, the wan woman in the looking glass, and the demonic soul caught on tape, a girl named Samara. It seems that Samara was abandoned and then killed by her adopted parents Anna and Richard Morgan. The adopted parents feared that Samara pushed her biological mother into madness. Samara's supernatural powers may have also led to the deaths of many horses.

Finally, Rachel locates where Samara was murdered and in the process Rachel becomes closer again with ex-boyfriend Noah, Aidan's father. Thereby, something positive has come about during this awful ordeal. The iconic image of the well in the forbidden video and the concept of the ring now become apparent. Adding to her terror, Rachel inadvertently descends the well shaft and becomes trapped inside. She comes upon Samara's corpse. The agent of the curse, Samara, has been met. Rachel escapes the well, notifies the authorities, and assures Samara's body a proper resting place. The decency of these actions, in Rachel's mind, should satisfy the restless spirit and the indomitable curse. The story, following such a climax, could have ended here.

Aidan's mother tells him that Samara has found peace and will leave them be. Rachel is startled to learn from him that Samara is still with them. Aidan shows the damaging marks scored by Samara on his arm. Rachel is stunned by this revelation. While Aidan's father Noah is working at home, his television comes on blasting static sound. When the television comes on a second time, Noah realizes he is doomed. The hypnotic image of the well dominates the screen. Suddenly, Samara pulls herself out of the hellish well and approaches the screen. In the next instant, she has jumped out of the television looking for her prey.

Because of Aidan's account to Rachel, Rachel fears that Noah is at risk. To her absolute horror, she discovers that Samara has already finished off Noah. At last, Rachel has solved the mystery of the Ring. Only by making copies of the video to injure others can one avoid the death sentence. Despite the spiritual complications, Rachel forces her son to make a copy of the tape and Verbinski ends his fable. Rachel has become a better mother, but her understandable moral compromise is disconcerting.

Admittedly, the film's elaborate synopsis strains the more lenient scrutiny and structure of most campfire ghost stories. We have seen many times before the heightened or transfixed child in the Val Lewton production of *Curse of the Cat People* (1944), William Cameron Menzies' *Invaders from Mars* (1953), and M. Night Shyamalan's *The Sixth Sense* (1999). A long tradition of supernatural children abductions in Japanese mythology underpins the essential mechanism that governs *The Ring* and *Ringu*. With this folklore, the missing child—deathly pale—reappears in hard-to-find locales.[7] The burden of *The Ring* does not fall on Aidan, but rests squarely on the shoulders of technology and the direction of the curse appears aleatory. It is the peculiar coupling of electronics and the anonymity of our society that perpetuates the film's notion of evil. Acknowledging that Samara's initial victimization had nothing to do with technology, *The Ring* contrives Samara's avenue of revenge through technology. This link is tenuous and a good many critics have seized on the point. Still, the film is extremely persuasive in transforming television and the home recorder into the world's most dangerous weaponry. In addition, *The New York Times* perceived *Ringu* to be superior in many ways and the reviewer faulted *The Ring* for losing the original film's "fear-of-girls strain."[8] To digress about our age of new media and illegal downloading, the hidden moral of the story might support anti-piracy laws and measures—at least to intellectually property attorneys.

In Suzuki Koji's novel, the journalist assumes that the spiritual animus on the damned video is a manifestation of the id; the question of how the curse began may be misplaced since such horror tales need not have a point of origin. Instead these tales, like fear personified, seem to exist outside of chronological logic.[9] The tools of horror in *The Ring* are wholly not original, but they do blend artistically to generate a deadly presence of fate and a new oppression from our home electronic entertainment. Built into this ghostly apparatus are reliable tropes such as the sacredness of the nuclear family, negligent adults having a second chance to redeem or rue their lives, and young children with arrested development manifesting psychic powers. Furthermore, audiences have already seen television menacing humanity in Steven Spielberg's *Poltergeist* (1982) and David Cronenberg's *Videodrome* (1983). The semiotic analysis of the demonic video within the film might delight or infuriate many graduate film schools in the country and spawn dozens of Ph.D. dissertations. Needless to say, there is the contrarian Marshall McLuhan interpretation about television: "The medium is the message." Our stupendous dependency on home viewing in this period of American life may be our great undoing. Unlike Samara, shrouded in sleek black hair and coiled to lunge, silent film clown Buster Keaton literally emerged from the screen in his production of *Sherlock, Jr.*(1924), happy only to amuse us with laughter.

Sin City (2005)

A punkish neo-*noir* film propped by push-up bras, high heel pumps, and vicious scowls in twirling choreography of mayhem, betrayal, and steroid brutality must have a reason for being. Graphic novelist Frank Miller initiated the comic book version of *Spin City* inspired by hard boiled American crime novels but hell-bent on revitalizing the genre.[10] Idiosyncrasies aside, Miller was more than reluctant to see an inaccurate, mediocre film adaptation of his legendary *Sin City* series. This reluctancy forced director Robert Rodriguez to shoot and edit a long segment to help sell the proposed project to Miller. The gambit worked quite well.[11] Miller enjoyed the short film of Miller's *The Customer is Always Right* and he implored Rodriguez to allow him to full involvement with the feature film. Rodriguez's concept incorporated mostly a colorless palette with digital backlot design techniques. In fact, Rodriguez was one of the first directors to film predominately on digital back-lot. Using a high definition digital camera and staging his cast in front of a green screen, imaginary sets, and landscapes could be plugged in, similar to a television weatherman gesturing to a blank wall. Further, although the production was filmed in color, Rodriguez then transformed every frame monochromatically. By accenting a touch of color on eyes or apparel, the production team was confident of capturing the essential comic book sensibility, and thrilling mainstream critics such as Roger Ebert of the *Chicago Sun-Times*.[12]

Rodriguez employed raw ingenuity to begin his directing work and funded his production costs through paid medical testing volunteer work. His first film, *El Mariachi*, cost $7,000 to make and went on to win the 1992 Audience Award at the Sundance Film Festival.[13] Rodriguez followed this with several more high action films and then cashed in with the popular *Spy Kids* (2001 and 2002) franchise.

Crediting the full directing team behind *Sin City* means attributing some action scene work by the dean of "grind house" films, Quentin Tarantino. Definitely, Tarantino's manic spirit hovers above the general mood and fashion of neo-*noir* or post-*noir* confectionary. Still, it was the principal partnership between Rodriguez and Miller that led to the finished film. Frank Miller's style and sensibility are interpreted into a consistent motion picture aesthetic. In R. C. Harvey's introduction to *Frank Miller: The Art of Sin City*, Harvey credits Miller for inventing a demi-monde ideally suited for the sordid storytelling: "All the so-called good guys are bad guys redeemed buy briefly by a momentary, scarcely understood impulse that might pass for goodness, save for its motive, vengeance."[14] The story embarks on a stylish balcony atop Basin City (Sin City). Using a prologue that unwraps like a one-minute television commercial, a handsome, well dressed male offers an elegantly chic female a cigarette. He then shoots her dead. We leave the high altitude of opulence and descend into the dark crevices of a depraved metropolis. The film did very well at the box office and with many critics.

John Hartigan is a grizzled cop hunting a child molester named Junior. The race is on to stop Junior before another rape. Hartigan, played with glee by Bruce Willis, gets no support from his gruff police partner, but Hartigan reaches Junior soon enough. Inflicting serious damage on Junior's genitals and other extremities, Hartigan cannot finish the job since the first double cross has Hartigan getting shot in the back by his partner. Hartigan remains incapacitated with a young girl as his sidekick.

Sin City pursues a wilder, second story about a massive goon named Marv, in love with a sex kitten Goldie. In a hotel bed they have torrid sex, but Marv wakes up to a corpse. The cops descend on the room a moment later. Marv fights his way out of the hotel and swears to seek Goldie's killer. At Lucille's home, he is cautioned about avenging Goldie. Lucille, you see, is Marv's parole officer.

At Kadie's Bar, Marv grabs any gossip he can before two thugs drag him into the alley. Overtaking them, Marv learns who dispatched them to Kadie's. Following a chain of clues, Marv reaches a debauched priest who hints that Junior's family is tied to Goldie's death. Rodriguez and Miller have now also tied story one to story two.

Marv murders the priest but is surprised by a beautiful Goldie lookalike who shoots him. Flinching in pain at this, Marv appears to be reenacting poorly to Jimmy Stewart's reaction to Kim Novak in the second half of *Vertigo* (1958). Marv questions his sanity, as well might the audience.

Arriving at Junior's rural family home, Marv discovers human remains. Creepy Kevin knocks Marv cold over the head. He comes to and spots the appalling sight of head trophies mounted on the wall. Inexplicably, Marv's parole office (now missing her hand) is in the scene and she announces Kevin's acts of cannibalism. Marv manages to free himself while Lucille is gunned down by a militia group. He soon learns that Junior's immediate kin, Cardinal Patrick Henry Roark ordered Goldie's death. This necessitates a trip to the tenderloin section of Old Town where Marv encounters Goldie's twin sister, Wendy. The street prostitutes torture Marv, which inadvertently becomes the price Marv must pay for more knowledge about Kevin and Goldie.

Incensed beyond reason, Marv beheads Kevin and brings this latest trophy to the Cardinal. Marvin is told that Kevin's ritual of dismembering and consuming whores were based on "spiritual purity." Apparently, Goldie found out about Kevin's secrets and posed a grave threat to Kevin and the Cardinal. Hearing more than enough, Marv murders the Cardinal. The Cardinal's staff takes aim at Marv and fire. Miraculously, Marv does not die and he is framed for too many deaths. We jump to death row where Marv receives Wendy for a conjugal visit. To take away the sexual surge of good feeling, the prison electrocutes Marv.

The film plot changes course abruptly to bartender Shellie, who is abused by ex-beau Jackie Boy. This segment is built on a love triangle for Shellie's new lover, Dwight, gives Jackie Boy a little push back. Jackie Boy is a cop but behaves worse than most of the thugs in Old Town. An inciting incident occurs when Jackie Boy brutalizes a young whore named Becky. Expert fighter Miho slices the hand off of Jackie Boy and finishes off Jackie Boy's gang. Although the prostitutes have humiliated Jackie Boy, the highly regarded truce between the police and the hookers is permanently shattered. Dwight carts the corpses to a tar pit and imagines that he's in dialogue with Jackie Boy's ghost. Thugs assault Dwight at the pit and run off with Gail who is Dwight's former lover.

Miho rescues Dwight while gang members (bearing Jackie Boy's severed head) evade Dwight. Adding to the grotesque horror is Gail's torture. As the situation turns to Dwight's advantage, he sends a proposition to Gail's tormentors: Jackie Boy's head for Gail's freedom. This leads to a final ambush in Old Town whereby the solidarity of the whores overwhelms the mercenary thugs and Dwight rekindles with Gail.

Looping back to the film's first tale (and journeying back in time before Marv's and Dwight's segments), Hartigan is convalescing and Junior's father—a senator—has harsh news for the aged police officer. The theme of framing an innocent man for a crime is played up again by Rodriguez and Miller. According to the senator, Hartigan will serve out Junior's prison time. The girl, Nancy, whom Hartigan saved from Junior's violence pledges to Hartigan that she will write him weekly during his incarceration.

After many years in prison, Hartigan fails to get another letter from Nancy but instead finds a finger in his mail. When Hartigan is released from jail, he seeks his old police buddy who reconciles with Hartigan. Sadly, Hartigan learns that his wife has walked away from his life. Hartigan, obsessed and believing that Junior's family has harmed Nancy, ferrets her out from Kadie's Bar. Nancy found employment there as a favorite stripper and she has all ten fingers.

Together at a hotel, Nancy declares strong feelings for her hero Hartigan. Intruding into their private world is a transformed Junior—disfigured and jaundiced. Junior manages to steal away with Nancy and pulverizes Hartigan. Indomitable Hartigan gives chase to Junior's farm where he subdues Junior once and for all. Hartigan is burning to expose the senator's rancid operation that is the blight of Sin City, but internal forces paralyze Hartigan, leading to his suicide. The film's epilogue has the young prostitute Becky from the Jackie Boy/Dwight segment leaving a hospital. She is accosted by the suave, handsome stranger from the prologue. He extends to her a cigarette.

The credibility of *Sin City's* story boarding for a mainstream audience is a laughable proposition to be sure. Miller's graphic novelization conforms to the rules of *noir* melodrama that are the hallmark of adult cartoons, dark Japanese anime, and violent video games. Miller's more recent graphic innovations can be seen in the art of elimination, knowing how much more he can leave out of the visual frame.[15] For avid film fans who cannot consume enough muscular aggression from the cinema of 'grind house', *Sin City* proffers raw sensation preserved faithfully and thoroughly graphically. Nearly every narrative detail in the film is hyperbolically unreal and politically incorrect, yet at the oddest moments *Sin City* sets an earthy tone of human dignity in the disgusting Basin. For traditional film purists who love Bogart and Bacall in Howard Hawks' classic *noir*, *The Big Sleep* (1946), there probably is no comfortable access into *Sin City*. Ironically, although sixty years separate these two highly praised films, America's tangled crime and birthright vice are unbothered by this flattering attention. Naturally, Rodriguez and Miller are at work on *Sin City 2*, rumored to be released in 2009.

Notes:

1. Taubin, Amy, *Village Voice review*, July 19-24, 2001.
2. John Cameron Mitchell (text) and Stephen Trask (lyrics), *Hedwig and the Angry Inch* (Woodstock: The Overlook Press, 2000), 43.
3. Elizabeth L. Wollman, *The Theatre Will Rock: A History of the Rock Musical from Hair to Hedwig* (Ann Arbor: The University of Michigan Press, 2006), 184-185.
4. J. P. Telotte, *The Cult Film Experience*, Gaylyn Studlar, *Midnight S/Excess: Cult Configurations of "Femininity" and the Perverse* (Austin: University of Texas Press, 1991), 143.
5. Judith A. Peraino, *Listening to the Sirens: Musical Technologies of Queer Identity from Homer to Hedwig* (Berkeley: University of California Press, 2006), 248.
6. Rick Worland, *Horror Film: An Introduction* (Malden and Oxford: Blackwell Publishing, 2007), 115-116.
7. Carmen Blacker, *Supernatural Abductions in Japanese Folklore* Asian Folklore Studies, Vol. 26, No. 2 (Nanzane University 1967), 111-115.
8. Elvis Mitchell, *The New York Times* review (October 18, 2002).
9. Jay McRoy, ed., *Japanese Horror Cinema*; Eric White, *Case Study: Nakata Hideo's 'Ringu' and "Ringu 2"* (Edinburg: Edinburg University Press, 2005), 45-46.

10. Milo George, ed., *The Comics Journal Library: Frank Miller* (Seattle: Fanta-graphics Books, 2003), 80-81.

11. Frank Miller and Robert Rodriguez, *Frank Miller's Sin City: The Making of the Movie* (Austin: Troublemaker Publishing, 2005), 17-18.

12. Roger Ebert, *Chicago Sun-Times review* (March 31, 2005).

13. Frank Miller, *Frank Miller: The Art of Sin City*; R. C. Harvey. *Introduction* (Milwaukee: Dark Horse Comics, 2002), i.

14. Miller, *Frank Miller: The Art of Sin City*; R. C. Harvey. *Introduction*, iii.

15. Robert Rodriguez, *Rebel Without a Crew: Or how a 23 Year Old Filmmaker with $7000 Became a Hollywood Player* (New York: Plume, 1996), 11.

Conclusion

It would be provocative and gratifying, if not sheer heresy, to teach a college history class built entirely on the backs of a century of cult films, yet a great deal of cultural history and exposé unfolds about America on screen irrespective of Hollywood's high gloss efforts towards patriotism and societal flatteries. *Reefer Madness* (1936), in all of its ludicrous inaccuracies about drug abuse and marijuana society, mirrored an impression of truth about the 1930s mores. Stanley Kubrick's *Dr. Strangelove* (1964) had a sure grip on the rapid pulse of this country looking into the brink of nuclear annihilation. Dennis Hopper and Peter Fonda's *Easy Rider* (1969) reinvested the American biker movie with a finely perceptive indictment of national intolerance, ignorance, and impotency. Perhaps *The Rocky Horror Picture Show* (1975), thirty years after the fact, lessened the initial disquietude regarding Dr. Alfred Kinsey's 1948 study that revealed prevalent homosexual practices in the United States. Darren Aronofsky's harrowing account of multi-generational drug abuse in *Requiem for a Dream* (2000) would serve as searing dialectic refrain to *Reefer Madness*. How resonant is the irony that the alcoholic (and anti-Semitic) star of the godless *Mad Max* trilogy astonished the film establishment by producing and directing the controversial, violent blockbuster, *The Passion of the Christ* (2004)?[1] In the final analysis, what does cinematic history tell us when the auteur of filth, John Waters, is celebrated on Broadway with a musical smash hit of his far gentler cult film *Hairspray* (1988) and is rewarded grandly with a big box office Hollywood version of the musical—starring John Travolta in the drag role created by the scandalous Divine? Divine, after all, had realized film immortality by eating fresh dog manure at the end of *Pink Flamingos* (1972). Susan Sontag dissects the matter of bad taste cogently in her famous collection of essays, *Against Interpretation: and Other Essays:* "I am strongly drawn to camp, and almost as strongly offended by it."[2]

Many notable cult directors bear mentioning as an appropriate acknowledgement to this volume's study: Dario Argento, Pedro Almodóvar, Woody Allen, Darren Aronofsky, Mario Bava, Ingmar Bergman, Kathryn Bigelow, Danny Boyle, Tim Burton, Stephen Chow, Joel and Ethan Coen, Sofia Coppola, Alex Cox, Stephen Elliott, Federico Fellini, David Fincher, Amy Heckerling, Jack Hill, Werner Herzog, Dennis Hopper, Allen and Albert Hughes, Jim Jarmusch, Spike Jonze, Kiyoshi Kurosawa, Stanley Kubrick, Spike Lee, Sergio Leone, Elaine May, Paul Morrissey, Terry Katsuhiro Otomo, Alan Parker, Rob Reiner, Nicolas Roeg, George Romero, Martin Scorsese, Susan Seidelman, Jim Sharman, Quentin Tarantino, Slava Tsukerman, Larry and Andy Wachowski, Wayne Wang, John Waters, Keenan Wayans, John Woo, and Terry Zwigoff.

As Umberto Eco notes astringently, "A cult movie is the proof that, as literature comes from literature, cinema comes from cinema."[3] While that observation holds a great deal of aesthetic truth, this canon of cinema art is first and foremost social x-ray. Cult attraction characterizes a variation of modern day anthropology. Our societal reflection is demystified in part due to the cult film artist's minority point of view. Current cult films, as a signifying constellation of sorts, are neither excessively deviant nor deceptive about our society in an age of greater sexual explicitness, commodification of vulgarities, and graphic displays of carnage and cruelty. In a culture that witnesses listlessly on the nightly news shocking photographs of torture from the American military-run Abu Ghraib prison in Iraq, cult films and independent cinema fare are far less radioactive and obscene. Living in relative transparency from the vantage point of *Life* and *Look* magazines in an America long forgotten since the 1963 Kennedy assassination, 1950s cult films internalized and inadvertently subverted our nation's greatest need to conserve our innocence. In stark contrast to this stance is the popular slew of contemporary cinema of violence as typified by *Se7en* (1995), *Saw* (2004), and *300* (2007). Michael Moore's success as an ironic, documentary filmmaker relies heavily on the cult movies' engines of personalized sarcasms and satirical broadsides found in *Atomic Café* (1982); clearly, Moore—political gadfly and prankster that he is—stands as the antithesis of quintessential senior documentary artist and social activist Frederick Wiseman.

The pure, unadulterated worship of film is firmly a realm of cult culture and the elite elements of cult film society expect some degree of esoteric understanding of the objects of worship. In this line of reasoning, cult films that are not widely known have greater pedigree and status for aesthetic chauvinists. Therefore, George Lucas' *Star Wars* franchise may be the most celebrated cult title in the world and fail to register at all in more rarefied circles of connoisseurship. Or to put this matter in another framework, the classic 1939 children's film *The Wizard of Oz* has added meaning to adult gay culture and also to underground drug culture. By removing the eternal, sacrosanct film soundtrack and including Pink Floyd's highly regarded concept album *Dark Side of the Moon* (1973), rock music enthusiasts encounter the "Dark Side of the Rainbow"—essentially a harsher reinterpretation of Dorothy's journey and the Wizard's semiotics, assisted by recreational pharmaceuticals and progressive rock invention. Again, this line of thought evokes another Umberto Eco notion on textual syllabus and *intertextual frames*, when things can be separated from the whole and transform a film into a cult object.[4]

When in the early 1980s the home video recorder reordered the public's ability to watch selected movies at home, cult film culture was irrevocably changed. The need to travel to a movie theatre was eliminated and the audience component was extracted from the cult film equation. The dimension of merging with an anonymous congregation was forsaken in a trade-off for the convenience of home viewing. This facet is far from frivolous. Although college campuses kept up the concept of hip "midnight film" showings, many cities and towns were losing art cinemas and repertory film theatres in the advent of the multiplex inside malls and suburban overdevelopment. That is why the 1991 Sarasota, Florida arrest of Pee Wee Herman (Paul Reubens) for masturbating publicly inside a pornographic movie theatre has an air of unreality. The children's cult TV star could have stayed at home unbothered and scandal-free with trashy VHS tapes.

Participatory cult films such as *Rocky Horror* and *Hedwig* are highly musical in concept and have had origins in live theatre; the carryover into large audience adulation is an easier argument against home viewing on DVD, VHS and cable television. Moreover, the powerful techno-fashion generated by YouTube and iPhone have transformed the notion of film production and consumption. The heyday of cult viewing ended a generation ago just as theatres were introducing "no smoking" and "no drugs" prohibitions in their balconies. On a national map, there are ample cities and college towns that maintain some programming for these sorts of films and many video stores have a cult films wall. In spite of that, as the decade concludes in this new century, too many new cult cinema devotees will not comprehend fully the historical end to the raw yet exculpated cult experience inside a theatre. A fifteen thousand dollar home entertainment system may give an owner certain bragging rights, but the cool graphite black equipment will never transport the gang back to Manhattan's gloriously ramshackle Elgin Theatre circa 1973—the Golden Age of Cult.

Notes:

1. Caryn James, *Film; No Such Thing as Bad Publicity*, *The New York Times* article (December 24, 2006).
2. Susan Sontag, *Against Interpretation: and Other Essays*, *Notes on "Camp"* (New York: Picador, 1961), 275.
3. Umberto Eco, *Travels in Hypereality* (San Diego, New York, London: Harcourt Brace Jovanovich, 1986), 199.
4. Eco, *Travels in Hypereality*, 200.

Bibliography

Agee, James. *Agee on Film: Criticism and Comment on the Movies.* New York: McDowell, Oblensky, 1958.

Barker, Martin, ed. *The Video Nasties: Freedom and Censorship in the Media.* London: Pluto Press, 1984.

Barrios, Richard. *Screened Out: Playing Gay in Hollywood from Edison to Stonewall.* New York: Routledge, 2003.

Beard, William. *The Artist as Monster: The Cinema of David Cronenberg.* Toronto: University of Toronto Press, 2006.

Blacker, Carmen. *Supernatural Abductions in Japanese Folklore.* Asian Folklore Studies, Vol. 26, No. 2. Nanzane University 1967.

Bloch, Robert. *Psycho.* New York: Tom Doherty Associates 1959. Gould, Jack. *TV: Why 'Bonanza'? The New York Times* feature. July 21, 1965.

Booker, M. Keith. *Alternate Americas: Science Fiction Film and American Culture.* Westport: Praeger Publications, 2006.

Bower, Anne L. ed. *Reel Food: Essays on Film and Food*; Claflin, Kyri Watson. *Jean-Pierre Jeunet and Marc Caro's Delicatessen.* New York and Abingdon: Routledge, 2004.

Braudy, Leo & Marshall Cohen, eds. *Film Theory and Criticism.* Sconce, Jeffrey. *'Trashing' the Academy: Taste, Excess, and Emerging Politics of Cinematic Style.* New York: Oxford University Press, 2004.

Brown, Allan. *Inside the Wicker Man.* London: Macmillan, 2000.

Bukatman, Scott. *Blade Runner.* London: British Film Institute, 1999.

Buñuel, Luis. *My Last Sigh: The Autobiography of Luis Buñuel.* New York: Vintage Books, 1984.

Cagin, Seth and Philip Dray. *Hollywood Films of the Seventies: Sex, Drugs, Violence, Rock 'n' Roll, and Politics.* New York: Harper, 1984.

Chibnall, Steve ed. *British Horror Cinema;* Hunt, Leon. *Necromancy in the U.K.: Witchcraft and the Occult in British Horror.* London and New York: Routledge, 2002.

Hutchings, Peter. *The Amicus House of Horror*; Chibnall, Steve, Ed. *British Horror Cinema.* London and New York: Routledge, 2002.

Cocteau, Jean and Ronald Duncan. trans. *Beauty and the Beast: Diary of a Film.* New York: Dover Publications, 1972.

Cocteau, Jean and Robert Phelps , Richard Howard, trans. *Professional Secrets, An Autobiography of Jean Cocteau.* New York: Evanston, San Francisco, London: Harper & Row, 1972.

Cocteau, Jean and Robert Phelps. *Professional Secrets: an autobiography of Jean Cocteau drawn from his lifetime writings.* New York: Farrar, Straus and Giroux, 1970.

Cocteau, Jean and Elizabeth Sprigge, trans. *The Difficulty of Being.* New York: Peter Owens Ltd and Editions du Rocher, 1967.

Cocteau, Jean. *Once Upon A Time—French Poet Explains His Filming of Fairy Tale* (DVD liner notes) Criterion Collection, 1998.

Cronin, Paul. *Roman Polanski: Interviews (Conversations with Filmmakers' Series).* Oxford: University of Mississippi Press, 2005.

Detweiler, Craig and Barry Taylor. *A Matrix of Meaning: Finding God in Pop Culture.* Grand Rapids: Baker Academic, 2003.

Doherty, Thomas. "The Exploitation Film as History: *Wild in the Streets." Literature/Film Quarterly* 12, no 3. (1984).

Dowdy, Andrew. *The Films of the Fifties: The American State of Mind.* New York: William Morrow, 1973.

Drazin, Charles. *Blue Velvet: A Bloomsbury Movie Guide.* New York: Bloomsbury Publication, 1998.

Dyer, Richard. *Se7en (BFI Modern Classics).* London: British Film Institute, 1999.

Ebert, Roger. *Chicago Sun-Times review.* March 31, 2005.

Eco, Umberto. *Travels in Hypereality.* San Diego, New York, London: Harcourt Brace Jovanovich, 1986.

Frasier, David K. *Russ Meyer—The Life and Films.* Jefferson, North Carolina and London: McFarland & Company, 1997.

Freedman, Jonathan and Richard Millignton, eds. *Hitchcock's American.* New York and Oxford, Oxford University Press, 1999.

French, Karl and Philip French. *Cult Movies.* New York: Billboard Books, 2000.

Fuiwara, Chris and Martin Scorsese. *Jacques Tourneur: The Cinema of Nightfall.* Baltimore: The Johns Hopkins University Press, 1998.

George, Milo, ed. *The Comics Journal Library: Frank Miller.* Seattle: Fantagraphics Books, 2003.

Gilman, Richard. *Decadence: The Strange Life of an Epithet.* New York: Farrar, Straus and Giroux, 1979.

Goldman, William. *Adventures in the Screen Trade.* New York: Warner Books, 1984.

Gunning, Tom. *The Films of Fritz Lang.* London: British Film Institute, 2000.

Hoberman, J. and Jonathan Rosenbaum. *Midnight Movies.* New York: Da Capo Press, 1983.

Hogle, Jerrold E. *The Undergrounds of the Phantom of the Opera.* New York and Hampshire, England: Palgrave, 2002.

James, Caryn. *Film; No Such Thing as Bad Publicity. The New York Times* article, December 24, 2006.

Jancovich, Mark, Antonio Lazaro Reboll, Julian Stringer and Andy Willis. eds. *Defining Cult Movies.* Manchester: Manchester University Press, 2003.

Lang, Fritz and Barry Keith Grant. *Fritz Lang: Interviews (Conversations with Filmmakers).* Oxford, Mississippi: University Press of Mississippi, 2003.

Leaming, Barbara. *Polanski, A Biography.* New York: Simon and Schuster, 1981.

Lentricchia, Frank and Jody McAuliffe. *Crimes of Art + Terror.* Chicago London: The University of Chicago Press, 2003.

Leroux, Gaston. *The Phantom of the Opera (Le Fantôme de l'Opéra).* New York: Grosset and Dunlap, 1911.

Maslin, Janet. *Film Festival Review; A Dangerous Game With Several Endings* (review of *Run Lola Run*). The New York Times, March 26, 1999.

McCarthy, Soren. *Cult Movies in Sixty Seconds.* London: Fusion Press, 2003.

McCarty, John. *Splatter Movies.* New York: St. Martin's, 1984.

McRoy, Jay, ed. *Japanese Horror Cinema*; White, Eric. *Case Study: Nakata Hideo's 'Ringu' and "Ringu 2."* Edinburg: Edinburg University Press, 2005.

Medved, Michael and Harry Medved. *The Golden Turkey Awards.* New York: Perigee/Putnam, 1980.

Mendik, Xavier and Graeme Harper. *Unruly Pleasures, The Cult Film and its Critics.* Guildford, England: FAB Press, 2000.

Miller, Frank. *Frank Miller: The Art of Sin City.* Harvey, R. C. *Introduction.* Milwaukie: Dark Horse Publishing, 2002.

Miller, Frank and Robert Rodriguez. *Frank Miller's Sin City: The Making of the Movie.* Austin: Troublemaker Publishing, 2005.

Mitchell, Elvis. *The New York Times review.* October 18, 2002.

Mitchell, John Cameron (text) and Stephen Trask (lyrics). *Hedwig and the Angry Inch.* Woodstock: The Overlook Press, 2000.

Morton, Ray. *King Kong: The History of a Movie Icon from Fay Wray to Peter Jackson.* New York: Applause Books, 2005.

Muller, Agnes C. ed. *German Pop Culture: How "American" Is It?* Kosta, Barbara. *Tom Tykwer's Run Lola Run and The Usual Suspects.* Ann Arbor: University of Michigan Press, 2004.

Palmer, Christopher. *Philip K. Dick: Exhilaration and Terror of the Postmodern.* Liverpool: Liverpool University Press, 2003.

Palmer, William J. *The Films of the Seventies: A Social History.* Metuchen: Scarecrow, 1987.

Peary, Danny. *Cult Movies.* New York: Dell, 1981.

———. *Cult Movies 2.* New York: Dell, 1983.

———. *Cult Movies 3.* New York: Fireside, 1998.

Peraino, Judith A. *Listening to the Sirens: Musical Technologies of Queer Identity from Homer to Hedwig.* Berkeley: University of California Press, 2006.

Quart, Leonard and Albert Auster, eds. *American Film and Society Since 1945.* Westport, CT and London: Praeger, 2002.

Rebello, Stephen. *Alfred Hitchcock and the Making of Psycho.* New York: St. Martin Press, 1990.

Richards, John H. *In the Little World: A True Story of Dwarfs, Love and Trouble.* New York: HarperCollins, 2001.

Riley, Philip J. *Phantom of the Opera (Hollywood Archives Series).* Absecon, New Jersey: MagicImage Filmbooks, 1999.

Rodley, Chris. *Cronenberg on Cronenberg.* London: Faber and Faber, 1992.

———. *Lynch on Lynch.* London: Faber and Faber, 1997, 2005.

Rodriguez, Robert. *Rebel Without a Crew: Or how a 23 Year Old Filmmaker with $7000 Became a Hollywood Player.* New York: Plume, 1996.

Royer, Carl and Diana Royer. *The Spectacle of Isolation in Horror Films: Dark Parades.* Binghamton: Haworth Press 2005.

Rudolph, Gray. *Nightmare of Ecstasy.* Los Angeles: Feral House, 1994.

Sammon, Paul M. *Future Noir: The Making of Blade Runner.* New York: HarperPaperbacks, 1996.

Samuels, Stuart. *Midnight Movies.* New York: Macmillan, 1983.

Sarris, Andrew. *Confessions of a Cultist: On the Cinema, 1955—1969.* New York: Simon & Schuster, 1970.

Scott, Ian. *American Politics in Hollywood Film.* Edinburgh: Edinburgh University Press, 2000.

Shapiro, Jerome. *Atomic Bomb Cinema: The Apocalyptic Imagination on Film.* New York and London: Routledge, 2002.

Sitney, P. Adams, ed. *Film Culture Reader.* New York: Praeger, 1970.

Sobchanck, Vivian. *Screening Space: The American Science Fiction Film.* New Brunswick, New Jersey: Rutgers University Press, 1999.

Sontag, Susan. *Against Interpretation: and Other Essays, Notes on "Camp."* New York: Picador, 1961.

Spicer, Andrew. *Film Noir.* Harlow, England: Pearson Education Limited, 2002.

Summers, Anthony. *Official and Confidential: The Secret Life of J. Edgar Hoover.* New York: G.P. Putnam's Sons, 1993.

Taubin, Amy. *Village Voice review.* July, 2001.

Telotte, J.P., ed. *The Cult Film Experience.* Austin: University of Texas Press, 1991.

Thomson, David. *The Alien Quartet: A Bloomsbury Movie Guide.* New York and London: Bloomsbury Publications, 1998.

Waller, Gregory A., ed. *American Horrors: Essays on the Modern American Horror Film.* Urbana: Univ. of Illinois Press, 1987.

Warren, Bill. *Keep Watching the Skies! American Science Fiction Movies of the Fifties Vol. 1.* Jefferson & London: McFarland, 1982.

Waters, John. *Crackpot: The Obsessions of John Waters.* New York: Macmillan, 1983.

Wollman, Elizabeth L. *The Theatre Will Rock: A History of the Rock Musical from Hair to Hedwig.* Ann Arbor: The University of Michigan Press, 2006.

Wood, Robin, ed. *The American Nightmare.* Toronto: Festival of Festivals Press, 1979.

Worland, Rick. *Horror Film: An Introduction.* Malden and Oxford: Blackwell Publishing, 2007.

Yacowar, Maurice. *Run Lola Run: Renn for your Life:* An Article from Queen's Quarterly. Vol. 106, Issue 4, December 1999.

Index